RELENTLESS POSITIVITY

A COMMON VETERAN BATTLING UNCOMMON ODDS

Rear Admiral Kyle Cozad
Retired Navy Pilot and Paralyzed Vet

Ballast Books, LLC
Washington, DC
www.ballastbooks.com

ISBN 978-1-955026-21-5

Library of Congress Control Number has been applied for

Printed in Hong Kong

Published by Ballast Books
www.ballastbooks.com

For more information, bulk orders, appearances or speaking requests,
please email info@ballastbooks.com

If your actions inspire others to dream more, learn more, do more, and become more—you are a leader.

—John Quincy Adams

CONTENTS

DEDICATION

Success is not final; failure is not fatal:
It is the courage to continue that counts.
—Winston S. Churchill

Several years ago, a close friend encouraged me to start writing a journal so that I could document my thoughts, my rehabilitation progress, and the major events I experienced during my recovery following a freak accident that left me paralyzed below the waist. At first, I balked at the thought, but when I finally gave in and began, I was surprised at how the project energized me. The more I wrote, the better it helped me understand and rationalize my struggle. After a while, this journal became more than just a day-by-day recount of my recovery. As you can imagine, this journey hasn't been an easy one for a guy who was fit and healthy one day and was told he'd spend the rest of his life in a wheelchair the next.

The inspiration of my immediate family, my friends, and my Navy family motivated me and kept my outlook positive during what some would argue could have been pretty dark days. What started out as a journal for my family has evolved into a larger story. I'm dedicating this collection of my experiences over the last several years to those whose inspiration has helped me grow stronger and stay motivated and has all but eliminated any thoughts of "I can't do that" from my vocabulary.

Although I didn't need to document my experience to realize this, there is one person whose love and support has been amazing in every sense of the word, helping to inspire me (or "drive" me, depending on your perspective) throughout this journey. My wife, Amy, has been there each and every day of this recovery. She's been there on the very difficult days and on those other days when we found ourselves laughing about things we never thought we'd be laughing about. She is the strongest lady I could ever imagine, and in addition to being the reason I count my steps, she's the reason that I work hard to get better every single day.

When I'm exercising at home or in one of many grueling physical therapy sessions, she teases me that if I keep improving like I have over the past several years, I'm going to have a chance to become a dancer someday. The only reason she tells me that is because she knows I've never been interested in dancing, but she finds it fun to tease me anyway. Despite that, I do know one thing: When I get to a point where I can dance again—not if, but when—I can't wait because my first dance will be with her!

CHAPTER 1

Don't Ever Give Up

*Don't give up. Don't ever give up! … Cancer can
take away all my physical abilities. It cannot touch my mind,
it cannot touch my heart, and it cannot touch my soul.
And those three things are going to carry on forever.*

—North Carolina State University
Head Basketball Coach, Jim Valvano

Fear gripped me unlike anything I had ever experienced before that night as I lay on the floor. I was terrified. Confused. I couldn't rationalize or comprehend why I couldn't move. Laying on the hardwood, I felt helpless for the first time in my life. I'm athletic and fit. *Why can't I stand up? Why can't I even move my legs?* My mind raced. *What the hell is going on?* I tried to roll over, but as hard as I tried to will my legs to work, they remained lifeless. My helplessness and confusion intensified. My heart raced, and my frustration mounted.

I shouted for my wife. "Amy!" It sounds stupid, but I yelled for her. "Just get me up, and I'll be okay. Amy!"

From that point, the rest of that night was a blur. My

adrenaline had kicked in as a result of the shock from the fall. Since I was in and out of consciousness, I have no memory of the EMS crew arriving and stabilizing me on a gurney. No memory of the ambulance ride across town. No memory of that night in the emergency room with dozens of x-rays and MRIs. I only remember a brief moment when I woke to find myself fully situated in the MRI with no idea why I was in that machine. As soon as I gathered enough awareness to recognize that I was in the MRI, the painkillers kicked in, and I once again lost consciousness.

That night changed my life forever. I am a naval officer and a naval aviator by trade. I'm not a psychologist by education or through practical experience, and I don't profess to be an expert in human behavior or individual motivational sciences. For that matter, I don't pretend to have a magic "message" tucked away in this book. Through documenting my experiences, I found a story to tell. My injury and the months of ongoing recovery have taught me a lot about myself, my faith, and my perspective that keeps the important things in life front and center.

The freak accident that evening resulted in broken vertebrae and paralysis below my waist. As a result, I have two large titanium rods, and as I half-heartedly tell people, enough screws surgically installed in my back between my L-2 and T-12 vertebrae to start a small home hardware store. The injury limited my mobility to a wheelchair, but over time with continued improvement, I now use a walker.

This story is a work in progress about my journey on what I hope will be a path to full recovery. I say that because I'm nowhere near finished working and improving on my physical condition and being fully independent. This story documents what has motivated me along the way and the people and things in my life that have helped me during some pretty challenging times. Equally important, it's about how I've approached my recovery during each and every difficult phase of my new normal.

Based on personal experience working with thousands of diverse people in my thirty-five-year career as a Navy pilot, I know that every individual reacts to the various challenges that life throws at them in very unique ways. Some people try to marginalize significant life events and act as if they've never happened. Others will simply dig in and just plain tough through any hard times that come their way. As an aviator, I had become used to compartmentalizing anything that might become a distraction to my ability to safely complete a mission or focus on an important project. But none of those approaches really seemed to apply as a single right answer to my specific life event.

So, I chose to share what you might consider a menu of coping mechanisms during some very difficult times. Since everyone copes with life's challenges differently, my approach to my injury and subsequent recovery won't resonate with everyone. There are many factors that have helped me stay positive during my recovery, just as there have been other elements that have helped pick me up during the inevitable hard times. Hopefully, in some small way, someone out there today who might be dealing with a similar situation—whether that pain is physical or emotional—can find a nugget or two of helpful insights from the things that have helped me along the way.

I've also included some of our personal progress updates that we posted on Caringbridge.org, a website devoted to helping people journal updates while experiencing a health crisis or situation. Only a day after my accident and surgery, friends and family inundated Amy and me with emails, texts, and phone calls for an update on what had happened and to pass along well wishes and prayers. We couldn't possibly have answered the hundreds of inquiries we received that first week, so Caring Bridge provided those steps of incremental progress that Amy and I have both made following my surgery. Many of the improvements have been physical, but others have been more psychological in nature. As I look back, it's given me a way to realize how much progress I've made in a relatively short time according to the experts. Hopefully, the Caring Bridge updates will add more of the personal aspects of how we tackled our progress, however deliberate and measured it has been.

I think it's fair to assume that I've had plenty of time over the past several years to think about where life has taken me. During my hospital stay for nearly six weeks immediately following the accident, I did a lot of thinking on a variety of life topics. During that time, I clearly realized how much in today's society we tend to get caught up in our day-to-day routines. So many people tend to fixate on things that distract them from the truly important things in their lives. Jobs, important hobbies, or even the powerful draw of social media can disrupt a predominant share of a person's time and focus in life.

This is only one man's opinion, but I'd venture to guess that, in many instances, those distractions eventually consume people to a point where they overshadow the important things that really matter. As a result of our cultural focus in today's society, I believe we come to take many things in life for granted. For me, I came to understand this in an intimate way as a result of my injury. The lessons I've learned throughout my journey have given me a new perspective on living life to its fullest, regardless of personal circumstances. I'm not even close to a full recovery—yet—but I consider myself a fighter. Yes, I've got a long way to go, but as I tell people every day, my story is a work in progress.

The thoughts in this book have helped remind and motivate me that, despite the circumstances, giving up and quitting is never, ever an option—at least it will never be an option for me. Regardless of how hard things get, despite how impossible the end goal might seem, and regardless of what others tell you that you won't be able to do, you have to keep fighting. With that in mind, I often think about those words of wisdom North Carolina State University basketball coach Jim Valvano shared in his incredibly powerful speech as he battled an aggressive cancer: "Don't give up. Don't ever give up!"

CHAPTER 2

Gym Rat

Remember that guy that gave up? Neither does anyone else.
—Author unknown

In my younger years, I happily earned the moniker of gym rat. I lived to play basketball, and everything else in my universe, like school, meals, and sleep, had to fit around time in a dozen different gyms in the metropolitan Las Vegas area. I not only craved my time on the court, but I also wanted to make my dad proud. So, I earned good grades and stayed out of trouble, and I knew that my hard work and solid performance during my previous junior varsity season had positioned me for a spot on the varsity team roster. Making the Chaparral High School varsity team became the most important thing in my life during the first semester of my junior year.

As a gym rat, there was naturally one place I'd be the Friday night before tryouts arrived: playing in a pickup game at the University of Nevada, Las Vegas sports and recreation complex. In the final game of the evening, I got tangled up chasing a loose ball and rolled my right ankle during a very awkward landing.

More than just a roll—I heard my cartilage pop, and the combination of pain and swelling became immediately unbearable. I flashed forward in my mind to varsity tryouts on Monday, which made the injury even more unbearable. Since I knew that I'd only make the varsity team by performing well during tryouts, I had to suck it up and keep going.

After I made my way home that evening, I immediately iced my ankle and watched the discoloration, discomfort, and swelling grow throughout the night. I fixated on missing tryouts and the unthinkable result of not making the team after all my hard work and practice. I lamented the potential lost opportunity to prove to the coach that I was ready to play competitively at the varsity level.

My father had also played basketball for his high school in a small town in Wyoming during the 1950s and later for a small teachers college in Nebraska, where he lettered and his teammates selected him as team captain during his senior season. Plain and simple, my dad knew everything about the game of basketball. Because of his knowledge of the game, he also knew about toughness. I could tell you a dozen or more stories about my father explaining how he played with broken bones and other significant injuries during his day. Although a high-school-aged boy doesn't always listen to everything his parents tell him, that's all I had to go on. So, I believed that's how ballplayers did things. I'd have to find the ability to tough it out and play through this sprained ankle to get my shot at the varsity team.

After I iced my ankle that Friday night, Dad pulled me out of bed early on Saturday because we had work to do. We lived in a new home at the time, and there always seemed to be plenty of work around the house. That day's work required landscaping—or, more accurately, digging deep holes in the earth's scorched surface comprising more rock and impacted clay than dirt. We'd dig the hole using a pickaxe and shovel, then load the rocks in our wheelbarrow. Dad always played the role of construction supervisor over me, his skilled laborer.

In retrospect, I'm not really sure whether this fell into Dad's definition of character building, toughing it out, or just plain old-fashioned hard work. Regardless of where it fell in the scheme of life, I hobbled around all day with my ankle taped tightly. Down the block we lived on, back and forth to the open desert, we dumped wheelbarrow after wheelbarrow of rock. The entire time, Dad convinced me that the more I walked it off, the better off I'd be.

By the end of the day, we had finished, and from the look of things, my ankle was finished too. It had become swollen and discolored and hurt to a point where I really couldn't place any weight on it.

With tryouts just a day away, my father did something out of character for him. He relented and finally said, "Let's go see a doctor." I knew I was in trouble after hearing that. Describing my dad as old school would be the understatement of the day. For him, medical care often consisted of one or two simple treatments: applying ice or heat (I never figured out whether he knew when to apply which) or rubbing dirt on a wound. Regardless of his treatment methods, "toughing it out" was always part of the medical prescription.

Nonetheless, we found a same-day appointment at a sports medicine clinic. After x-rays and a thorough physical exam, the verdict came in. I had suffered a severe sprain, and the doctor said that I was lucky to avoid having a discussion about surgery to correct the cartilage damage that had been done. The doctor knew I had a full basketball season in front of me, and he felt confident that he could treat me without surgery. So, he prescribed the lesser of two medical evils: physical therapy for a week.

The funniest part of the story was when the physical therapy tech asked me how my injury had happened. He expressed concern about the significant discoloration and swelling—much more than he'd expect to see resulting from a simple sprain. I sheepishly admitted that I had tryouts coming up and that, as any athlete focused on attaining a goal likely would have done, I had tried to walk it off. He laughed and asked, "Who in the world convinced you to do that?" When I told him what my father had me doing over the weekend, he laughed even more loudly and admitted that he'd had the same sort of father who had prescribed something similar while he'd still lived at home. With his years of education and practical experience treating injured athletes, he convinced me that, in medical terms, not everything in life was as simple as being able to walk it off.

For the record, I made the team despite missing tryouts. For the first time in my life, I celebrated the fact that Mom and Dad were right. Hard work does pay off, even when you suffer an injury and miss varsity tryouts. Equally important, I also realized that, in the big scheme of life, you can't always walk it off.

CHAPTER 3

What Do You Want to Do with Your Life?

Optimism is the faith that leads to achievement.
Nothing can be done without hope and confidence.

—Helen Keller

The hours and hours I spent every day in the gym and my hard work in the classroom helped provide a discipline that carried over into my adult life. I'm a retired naval officer, fortunate to have risen to the rank of rear admiral over a thirty-five-year naval career that took me to some amazing places and provided some incredibly unique opportunities for me, my wife, and my children.

I received my commission from the United States Naval Academy in Annapolis, Maryland. As an unlikely ensign and prospective naval aviator from Las Vegas, Nevada, I had worked hard to earn the right to walk across the graduation stage on May 22, 1985, in Navy Marine Corps Memorial Stadium. To have my diploma and commissioning certificate delivered by President Ronald Reagan and shake the hand of a man who consistently demonstrated personal toughness and fortitude is a moment that I will never forget.

A few years prior, President Reagan had suffered a bullet wound to the chest at close range by a deranged assassin outside of the Washington Hilton Hotel. My graduating class remembered how he'd bravely bounced back from that attack with grace and humor. The honor of having him there would shape the service of my 900 or so graduating classmates who planned to make their mark as ensigns in the United States Navy or as second lieutenants in the United States Marine Corps. As tradition would have it, the guest of honor typically joins the Naval Academy superintendent—the senior officer assigned to the Naval Academy—to congratulate the top 100 graduates. However, I was nowhere near the top 100 of my classmates in order of merit.

The United States Naval Academy is a college unlike all others. The Academy requires the student body, or Brigade of Midshipmen, to study a rigorous academic curriculum with mostly engineering-focused majors that trend upwards of twenty semester hours as the standard. In addition to that rigorous academic program, each freshman must memorize a variety of professional requirements, such as the types and missions of ships, submarines, and aircraft, or have knowledge of current political and military events. Add those rigors to required formations prior to every meal and mandatory lights out for freshmen at 10:00 each evening, and it's easy to see how, before long, I ran out of hours in the day. However, that crazy schedule and time commitment didn't factor in basketball workouts. To say that I had a tough time in the classroom was like saying my dad's just-walk-it-off medical diagnosis of my ankle was just what the doctor ordered.

At any rate, I worked hard to achieve a balance in the classroom with my other military duties and on the basketball court, but I reached a point where I had to make a tough decision. Everyone's heard of athletes who suffer injuries at some point in their career, hurt for a few weeks, and get back in the lineup. However, some injuries are career ending. The Washington Redskins quarterback Joe Theismann suffered one of the most visibly disturbing career-ending injuries on national TV, and as a result, he had to medically retire from professional football. I, on the other hand, struggled to achieve an acceptable grade point average in the classroom, and that threatened my career. I held my breath every time the phone rang during my first Christmas break at home with my family since reporting to the Academy some six months earlier. I was convinced that I'd receive a call that would summon me back to Annapolis a week before our holiday break ended to face the wrath of the one process every midshipman feared—the dreaded academic review board.

Thankfully, that call never came, but then again, neither did an improved GPA. Shortly after the beginning of my sophomore year, my company officer—an officer in the regular Navy charged with a number of cadets—summoned me to his office. Although that sounds cordial, at the Academy, that was an order and not a social invitation. I put on my best uniform as thoughts of "What did I do?" or more importantly, "What did I get caught doing?" crossed my mind. My company officer was direct and to the point.

"Midshipman Cozad, do you like being here?"

I thought about this one for a minute. Was it a trick question? Nobody really likes their freshman year at any of the service academies. But, even if it was a trick question, telling my company officer "No, not really" was definitely not in my best interest.

Quickly reverting to survival mode, I blurted out, "Yes, sir. It's not what I thought it would be, but…"

He interrupted, "That's what I thought. And I'm curious—do you have any aspirations of a career in the NBA somewhere in your future?"

I did not have to think about that. I played as a fairly regular starter on the junior varsity team, but I was realistic that I didn't have a whole lot beyond Navy basketball.

"No, sir! I only want one thing. I want to be a Navy pilot."

After some further discussion—not a negotiation but really only a one-way conversation during which I was clearly in the receive mode—I quickly realized what had just happened. Unlike the medically retired Joe Theismann after his career-ending injury, I fell into another, much different category. As the company officer dismissed me and I jogged back to my room (the Academy does not allow us to walk in our massive dorm), I realized that I had just been academically retired. No more basketball. My grades had to become my priority so I could work toward graduation and the thing I wanted most: a quota for the Navy's flight school in a place considered to be the mecca of naval aviation—Pensacola, Florida.

Fortunately, that come-to-the-mountain talk with my company officer served to refocus my attention for the next three years. As a result, I graduated with a commission as an ensign in the United States Navy on that muggy, humid day in 1985. Elated just to graduate and receive my commission, I had no expectation of shaking the President's hand reserved for the top 100 merit graduates of my class. To tell the truth, I was just thankful to walk across the stage to receive my diploma that day.

But back to President Reagan. It was clear to every member of the class of 1985 that our Commander in Chief was a leader whose example we should all strive to measure up to. Considering his age, busy schedule, and recovery from a bullet wound to the chest just a few years prior, President Reagan could have taken a seat when offered after shaking the hand of the top 100 graduates. Instead, he shook his head and stood his ground. Despite what we can only imagine as taxing effort, President Reagan remained standing for the entire ceremony, shaking the hand of every single midshipman in the United States Naval Academy's class of 1985—including Midshipman Kyle Cozad. That demonstration of toughness and pure grit from our President and my Commander in Chief has never escaped me.

CHAPTER 4

Fly, Fight, Lead... and WIN!

*When people ask me what do I want to be remembered for,
I have one answer. I want the people to remember me as
a winner, 'cause I ain't never been nothing but a winner.*

—Coach Paul "Bear" Bryant

One could say that, despite a dubious academic beginning at the Naval Academy, things seemed to work out for me during what many of my classmates probably considered an unlikely career. Frankly, I never intended to stay in the Navy beyond my initial commitment. The mere thought of flying for a career had been an inspiration ever since the day a good friend took me to visit his squadron at Nellis Air Force Base in Las Vegas. I couldn't understand why some people chose to work in seemingly boring and benign careers such as law, accounting, or architecture. I had no desire to pursue that but rather sought a path toward aviation—and military aviation at that—as a means to put food on the table and, in retrospect, cheap beer in the refrigerator.

Little did I realize I'd soon replace that beer with diapers and baby formula! That single day with my friend on the flight line made my decision. I had the aviation bug, and I had it bad.

Thinking back to that discussion with my company officer during my sophomore year, I remain dissatisfied with the final direction that conversation took. However, refocusing on the classroom and keeping my nose above the proverbial minimum GPA mark earned me a slot at the Navy's flight school located in Pensacola, Florida. The Navy sends every budding flight student to a single location in Pensacola, where they begin their journey that will someday lead to earning their coveted wings of gold. Since every one of those hopeful future aviators passes through Pensacola on their aviation journey, it is affectionately known as the "Cradle of Naval Aviation."

Once I realized what I truly wanted to do in the Navy, flying drove every decision I made during my time in Annapolis. It drove my study habits, it drove the classes I took, and it drove every thought about how and when I'd get to Pensacola. However, man can't live on aviation alone, and I rationalized that many good pilots have equally good copilots.

Enter Amy Louise Welter. I met my future wife during my last week of summer vacation going into my senior year at the Academy. If there is any such thing as love at first sight, I was certain that I had found it. We met in Georgetown when I had chosen at the last minute to skip out on another party and head into the big city for an impromptu albeit low-key birthday celebration with another classmate of mine. Amy also happened to be out that night with a friend, and as her story goes, she "accidentally" locked her keys in her car. I have a suspicion that, shortly after meeting me, she pretended to go use the restroom but instead intentionally locked her keys in her car to play the damsel in distress to my knight in shining armor. A pretty extreme measure to spend a few more minutes with me that night, I must admit—but that's pure speculation on my part.

Regardless of how those keys got locked in her car, I took advantage of the situation and did what any aspiring aviator would do. I let my buddy unlock her car while I chatted Amy up and secured her phone number. We married just under a year later and have grown closer and closer with every day that we've been together since then. As a matter of fact, I later laminated the parking receipt that Amy gave me with her name and phone number handwritten on the back as a sentimental keepsake. I carry it in my wallet to this day as a treasured memento and reminder of that warm, August evening when we met and our love started. For decades, I've ensured it's made the transition from one wallet to another, believing that it just might continue to bring me good luck. It hasn't failed me yet.

No matter whose version of the how-we-met story you believe, we had our wedding at the Naval Academy Chapel several months after graduation, and within a few weeks, I was headed to Pensacola for initial aviation training. As we packed all our worldly belongings into the car, I could hardly contain my excitement with the understanding that our journey in naval aviation would soon begin.

There is something much bigger about naval aviation that transcends the allure of flight that I didn't understand until well after my training. Frankly, there are some things I don't think I fully understood or appreciated until I retired some thirty-five years later. As a rule, naval aviation is an unforgiving profession. There are rarely earned do-overs with dire life-or-death consequences that revolve around individual decision-making as it pertains to hundreds of sequences flown in a given mission. For example, a few things involved are precise interpretation of a multitude of spatial and contextual presentations that happen on every flight; an in-depth technical knowledge of the aircraft and weapons systems and how they are employed in a variety of good and bad scenarios; and, finally, the ability of one person (or one crew) to harness their peak level of performance each and every time they suit up to fly.

While the professionalism and application of those physical piloting skills in the world's most sophisticated aircraft are often referred to as airmanship, I always preferred the term my initial flight instructor used with me. During one of the first briefs, he laid things out for me, plain and simple.

"Ensign Cozad, I don't care how well you know your procedures. I don't care how well you know your aircraft operating limits. Don't get me wrong, it's a package deal, and you need to know them all cold anytime, anywhere. But just about anyone can commit words and procedures to memory. What separates great pilots from all the others are the monkey skills. You've got to be a good stick to be the best. And when you're the best, you'll be able to do this—that is, to fly Navy aircraft—for many years to come."

During flight school, things come fast. You're expected to master a range of topics from aerodynamics to meteorology to aircraft emergency procedures. You're expected to know mechanical aircraft systems cold. One minute, you're getting graded on how accurately you can describe how a molecule of fuel goes from the fuel cell until it's combusted; the next minute, you are describing how to avoid heavy weather in a variety of meteorological scenarios. You're expected to commit critical procedures to memory and to apply those procedures as you are flying, communicating via radio and interpreting the radio beacon signal after your instructor has pulled the controlling circuit breaker and rendered that signal inoperative.

That pace of one evolution after another rattled my nerves. Consider a syllabus that teaches someone how to taxi a high-performance aircraft on their first flight and accelerates them to a point where, fourteen flights later, they earn the right to fly solo. Then, on the second time, they must complete a complex set of aerodynamic maneuvers. No, they're not Blue Angels worthy, but that's an amazing learning curve to comprehend in two weeks' time. Throw in hot summer days, aircraft exhaust, a bit of student anxiety, and perhaps some initial airsickness, and I came to an easy conclusion—this is what I wanted to do for the rest of my career.

In aviation, and more specifically in naval aviation, there is no such thing as a perfect flight. They simply don't exist. Even the world-famous Blue Angels, the Navy Flight Demonstration Squadron, take the pursuit of the elusive perfect flight to an unparalleled level. The Navy's Blue Angels epitomize excellence in every practice and public airshow during a typical season. While the Navy and our general public recognize them as a symbol of aviation precision and excellence, the team refuses to accept any airshow or practice without excruciating self-criticism, all with an aim toward being better during the next show.

Often, that need for improvement is not apparent to the typical aviation enthusiasts who watch their shows, but that relentless pursuit of perfection is a common theme that permeates the rest of naval aviation. It's never just good enough. We all want to be better at what we do today than we were yesterday.

As much detailed planning as one might do, something always changes, and in many cases, some things just plain go wrong. Sometimes, it's a simple mistake that we make, such as missing a radio call from an air traffic controller, forgetting a checklist item on climb out, misinterpreting route flight clearance changes, or dealing with aircraft systems that don't always work as advertised. During flight school, it's an out-and-out battle (at least it seems that way for every student) between the instructor and the student. The instructor wants to create confusion. The instructor wants to overload a student's meager ability to multitask. The instructor wants to add a variety of distractions that inject the fog of war.

Although I didn't necessarily give my instructors credit for the method to their madness, I later realized that in doing those things, they were preparing me to succeed. They were setting the conditions for what I've come to call "dynamic resilience" or the ability to adapt, overcome, and perform at the highest level possible regardless of the challenges that any one pilot or crew will face on any given flight. At the end of the day, naval aviation is called upon to deliver firepower on the adversary. Nobody will care about your excuses or alibis, but they will take notice if and when you fail to deliver ordnance that might be required to preserve the safety of troops on the ground.

Naval aviation is an unforgiving profession, demanding your best on every flight. Having said that, every step of training—a never-ending requirement throughout one's career—requires that when you make a mistake or fail in any small measure, you have the resilience and the confidence to get back in the cockpit the very next flight to fly the best mission you've ever flown. Many naval aviators have never experienced failure in any measure, including falling short of a personal goal. Many have never been anything less than the best in the classroom, on the court, or on the field. But although none of us like to admit it, we learn to be better through those instances in which we fall short.

Naval aviation breeds competition. I'll be the first to acknowledge that, regardless of the aircraft one flies, we're all stereotypical Type A personalities. We like to win. We like to be better than our peers. We compete at everything. Simply put, we all want to be the best. Period. To be the best, most of us put in the time, effort, and physical preparation to be better than the guy or gal next to us. I know for some that sounds like an elitist club of egomaniacs, but it's not. In our profession, mistakes cost lives. It's our culture to expect to be the very best and to work hard to achieve that—every time we get in the cockpit! Naval aviation makes no apologies and demands we think and act like that every single day.

Having said that, naval aviation also breeds an incredible camaraderie and exceptional group of individuals with equally incredible egos who exemplify teamwork to the highest levels. Think about my description of the flight instructor methodically working to find the limits of your performance. That instructor prepared candidates to become the best individual aviator they could possibly be.

Once I earned my coveted wings of gold in the fall of 1986, my training had only begun. The Navy had created a reasonably proficient individual pilot, but I was headed to a community that depended on a large crew to hunt, find, and kill enemy submarines. Yes, I could fly an instrument approach down to minimums while handling compound emergencies, but it was now time to work with a team to accomplish complex missions.

Learning how to be part of a high-functioning team involves the next level in the pursuit of aviation excellence, whether that's a large crew on a multi-crewmember aircraft or a section or division of single piloted jets. The ability to merge multiple individual responsibilities that contribute to deliver a complex mission takes time, practice, and more practice. That mission execution must deal with the curveballs associated with weather, aircraft systems, and mechanical malfunctions, but it all comes together with the same precision and professionalism that our undergraduate flight school delivers for each individual pilot or flight officer who earns their wings. It also creates a bond and a culture of teamwork and trust in others to do their job, unrivaled in many other fields.

One of the best illustrations of the unique bond among naval aviators comes from a true story of two very different young pilots who came from two very different backgrounds during the Korean War. Jesse Brown, the son of a sharecropper in Mississippi, grew up with meager possessions. He graduated from high school and attended Ohio State University before pursuing his dream to fly Navy. Brown achieved his goal and became the Navy's first African American pilot in 1948. By comparison, Tom Hudner hailed from a middle-class family in Massachusetts. Not wealthy by any means, Hudner's family lived a comfortable lifestyle compared to that of Jesse Brown.

Hudner and Brown both met in their initial fleet squadron, VF-32, flying the F4U-4 Corsair. In a society where discrimination prevailed through many parts of the country, Brown and Hudner served as squadron mates that depended on each other to plan and fly complex missions against the enemy. They implicitly trusted each other to be the best at what they did, regardless of skin color. That trust personified the culture and spirit of teamwork in naval aviation formed by our common mission.

On December 4, 1950, on a mission during the Battle of Chosin Reservoir over North Korea, hostile fire struck Jesse Brown's F4U Corsair, likely rupturing an oil line and crippling his aircraft during a search-and-destroy mission. Unable to return to his aircraft carrier, Brown notified other squadron aircraft and continued his mission, although he'd been hit and needed to ditch his aircraft behind enemy lines. After his forced landing on the side of a snowy mountain, the fuselage pinned Brown's leg underneath his stricken aircraft.

Circling above the crash site, Hudner witnessed the wreckage below and the fire that engulfed Brown's Corsair. I can't speculate on his thoughts, but through his subsequent actions, I think it's fair to assume that the instincts bred in flight school and during his initial squadron tour took over and the engrained concepts of teamwork and "taking care of his wingman" kicked in. He didn't think twice about possible repercussions. He didn't think twice about landing in hostile territory. And he didn't think twice about the color of his friend's skin or where he had grown up. Hudner made a split-second decision based on instinct and the culture in which he had been trained as a naval aviator to crash land his own plane and race over to render whatever assistance he could offer to his stricken wingman.

Brown passed in and out of consciousness as Hudner worked to save him. A rescue helicopter arrived to assist, but they were unable to save their friend. Although historians capture Hudner's concern over a court-martial for willfully crash landing his aircraft and defying orders for his unselfish and heroic actions, Congress recognized Hudner with the Medal of Honor years later for "exceptionally valiant actions and selfless devotion to a shipmate." To this day, I think about the selfless consideration to put one's life at risk and to help a "wingman" as the epitome of what it means to be part of a team. Naval aviation helped form that bond as well as Hudner's instinct to help under the direst of circumstances.

I often think about who we are and what we stand for as naval aviators. We are more than the perception of an overly competitive group of good-looking, cocky, Type A personalities around whom the world revolves. (Okay, there are a few of those guys out there.) Our stellar training and the grading of every completed evolution has branded our identity. We learned through an incredibly arduous training regimen to be tough and to never give up. We've learned that resilience is a critical component of winning in the direst of circumstances. And we've learned the importance of teamwork in everything we do. Those who think they can win on their own are often singled out and don't make it very far in the profession of naval aviation.

In June of 2016, I had the incredible honor of officiating as the senior naval aviator at a winging ceremony at Naval Air Station Whiting Field, just east of Pensacola. Every winging ceremony is special. It's the culmination of undergraduate flight training, and the pride in personal accomplishment and pure energy exuded by the Navy, Marine Corps, and Coast Guard's newest aviators is hard to accurately describe in words. It's the formal rite of passage that serves as the steppingstone for each and every naval aviator as they prepare to take their place in the fleet. Traditions have changed a bit since I received my wings in 1985, but for the most part, the event still stands as one that most aviators compare only to the day they get married or the day their first child is born.

When I winged, each prospective naval aviator got his wings pinned on during an appropriately solemn ceremony, but it wasn't official until afterward, when each person was given a pitcher of beer to down. At the bottom of that pitcher, they'd find their shiny new wings of gold. To make things official, they'd finish their pitcher of beer and artfully guide those new wings to capture them in their teeth. I'm not 100 percent sure, but after doctors x-rayed a poor young guy and found his shiny new wings stuck in his esophagus, I think the Navy discontinued that tradition. The poor guy didn't get the full brief on how you were expected to catch those wings in your teeth.

That June 2016 winging ceremony that I officiated was especially meaningful to me. I beamed with pride as I pinned the same wings that Amy had pinned on my chest for the first time in 1985 on my son. For those wondering, yes, they were the same wings I caught in my teeth after drinking my pitcher of beer. I could see how my son had learned the same lessons of toughness, resilience, resourcefulness, and teamwork that I had learned many years ago. Not only did he learn them along the way—it was clearly part of his new identity as a naval aviator. It's an identity that remains yours for eternity and serves as the foundation of character for those fortunate enough to be called naval aviators.

CHAPTER 5

Life's Choices

Our lives are the summation of the choices we make—
not what happens to us but the choices we make about
what happens to us. God gives us the gift of free will.
The exercise of free will is what we all get.

—Vietnam POW (seven years) CDR Porter Halyburton

I worked hard during flight school. Although I might not have been the most naturally talented pilot in my class, I worked my butt off on each and every written test, graded simulator, or flight. Due to that hard work, I felt on top of the world when my wife, Amy, pinned on my coveted wings of gold in Corpus Christi, Texas, in October 1986. At that point in life, I focused inwardly on a couple of things: One, spending as much time with my new bride as the Navy would allow. Two, leveraging my new trade into a lucrative career with the airlines once I'd built enough flight time in my logbook and satisfied my original commitment to the Navy. For a young pilot, those two seemed to go together quite nicely.

I was excited to get my first choice of aircraft selection

alternatives. Being a tall guy who never really liked wearing a flight helmet during my initial flight training, I selected the maritime pipeline, which led to future duties flying the P-3 Orion. Several things influenced my desire and, ultimately, this decision. The Orion is a large, multi-engine, land-based aircraft that had the primary role of detecting and tracking Soviet submarines that began during the Cold War. I liked several aspects of that mission. We flew at high altitudes with a crew of eleven: three pilots, two navigators, two flight engineers, and several enlisted sensor operators. With the exception of practicing putting on our parachutes, we had no jump training but did have fairly extensive survival training for land and sea. In the Orion, we not only found and tracked submarines, but we also carried a complement of torpedoes, missiles, and mines.

In addition, the multi-engine makeup of that aircraft lent itself nicely to that airline transition that I fully expected in the not-so-distant future. The fact that the Navy uses the Orion as a land-based aircraft didn't break my heart either, even though, like any other naval aviator, it was always my dream to land on the aircraft carrier. Since the Orion was a large, land-based aircraft, I wouldn't have the opportunity for those carrier landings, as we deployed and conducted all of our training and readiness requirements from home base as opposed to packing up for periods of extended at-sea deployment time. My peers who flew jets and helicopters trained at sea—away from their families for weeks and months at a time. Mind you, I didn't hate the thought of going to sea—after all, I was in the Navy—but I found contentment with that new maritime community I'd joined. Amy shared that same commitment.

As I completed my transition training where I learned to fly the P-3, I discovered that the squadron to which the Navy had assigned me was scheduled for a six-month deployment shortly after my planned arrival. Specifically, they would be deployed to a small base in Iceland, called Keflavik, where squadrons had ready access to patrolling Soviet submarines in the Northern Atlantic. I was all in, eager to learn the crafts of anti-submarine warfare and do what every pilot wants to do: fly, fly, and fly some more! Amy, on the other hand, quickly learned what folks meant when they often cited the fact that the toughest job in the Navy is that of the Navy spouse.

We expected our first child in the months that my squadron had scheduled deployment and also planned a move to our next home in Maine. Around that time, I overheard a discussion between Amy her mom that confused me. As I listened in, half pretending not to hear their conversation, Amy confessed to her mom that she wasn't sure how she was going to handle traveling with me on deployment, storing furniture while we were gone, and then having a baby to boot. I gulped and tried to figure out where that massive communication failure had spiraled uncomfortably out of control. I hadn't been married long, but I had been married long enough to realize that most (if not all) miscommunications were my fault. The sooner I acknowledged that and jumped right to the "I'm sorry" part, the better off I'd be.

So, as soon as they finished, I said, "We have to talk." Of course, I began with, "I'm sorry. There seems to be a mix-up, and I'm sure it's my fault. Sweetheart, you are not going with me on deployment. You don't have a choice. You have to stay here with the other wives and hold down the home front until we get back in the spring."

A long, uncomfortable silence ensued. I watched the wheels turning in her head. She was—and continues to be—a thick-skinned, nothing-can-faze-me-and-nothing-can-stop-me kind of girl. She came back with a nonchalant, "That's okay. I'll be fine here by myself."

However, I could tell she had questions, and I had to ask her how she came to the assumption that she'd just pack things up and go on deployment with me. My new bride, soon-to-be mother of our first child, and brand-new Navy wife had come to the incorrect conclusion that, since my squadron was not attached to an aircraft carrier airwing and was technically considered land based, she'd be hopping the globe with me. Looking back, it still makes me smile when I think about how young and naive we both were.

For the record, during that first deployment, Amy learned her share of the toughness and resilience that characterizes Navy spouses throughout their service. Little did either of us know how many times that toughness and resilience would be called upon in the years to come.

During that initial assignment in Maine, we experienced three deployments and were blessed with each of our three children. I wish I could tell you we had triplets, but I believe it's more accurate to call them Irish triplets since they were all born just over a year apart. Ironically, the timing coincided with each of our deployment homecomings. The good news is that we figured out that math before we had any more.

In addition to the blessing of three healthy babies, we both really loved our squadron and our life of service. Yes, deployments were hard on the family, but very few things worthwhile in life come easily. We loved the camaraderie and the other like-minded couples who shared in similar journeys. We had a sense of family with the squadron and a fierce and loyal bond that allowed us to draw near and help one another through life's inevitable hardships.

Personally, I couldn't get enough of flying. I continued to work hard in various secondary duties and prided myself on knowing the P-3 inside and out. As a result, my leaders rewarded me with every qualification in the plane I could earn. Yet as much as I loved flying operational missions and training our younger pilots during instructional flights, I still had my eye on the airlines. I guess, at that point, the number of diapers and bottles of baby formula I could afford to buy on a big airline salary interested me more.

About the time I would need to begin my formal transition to the airlines and get serious about tendering my resignation from active duty, Amy and I found ourselves in Canada, where I worked as an exchange pilot on assignment to the Canadian Air Force. Living abroad in Nova Scotia made for an incredible experience for our young family—more flying and instructing for me, and as an added bonus, no deployments. In Canada, we measured time away from the family in days on short trips every now and then as opposed to months of predictable deployments. We traveled the country, took advantage of local attractions, and made lifelong friends.

I specifically recall one beautiful Saturday in the fall when I started a woodworking project in our garage early in the morning. It's not unusual for me to lose my sense of time when I really get involved in a project. When my good friend, who also happened to be on exchange from the UK, came over with a beer just after lunch, I decided to take a break. We settled into some Adirondack chairs on our front lawn and enjoyed a perfect autumn afternoon telling stories.

Remember the camaraderie that typically defines an aviation squadron or small military community? We had that in spades during that tour in Canada. So, one beer with a friend turned into five friends when we were joined by others out walking their dogs or diverting after taking out the garbage. Those five turned into twelve, and soon we had a block party replete with wives, kids, and yes, more beer. Friends would come and go, but those who had other things to do would return when they came back home.

Ultimately, what started as two close friends enjoying a beer on a quiet fall afternoon ended at about 3:00 a.m. when we ran out of bread and eggs. A local delicacy of toad in the hole was evidently a perfect Canadian nightcap. For those uninitiated, a toad in the hole is simply a piece of bread with a two-inch hole cut in the middle and an egg cracked into the hole. Throw that in a hot skillet for a few minutes, and you're in heaven! Once we ran out of groceries—and beer—folks reluctantly called it a night and retreated to the comforts of their own homes.

That night served to reinforce something for Amy and me. As much as I had planned and worked toward competitive employment in the airline industry, we had many friends who told us that life in the airlines wasn't the same as life within the naval aviation family that we'd adopted several years earlier. One of the best descriptions I heard about life in the airlines was that it tended to be more transactional and less relationship based. Sure, you had close friends, but the relationships and friendships that were forged through hardship, separation, and some great times served to make me question what I really wanted to do next.

Returning to my days playing basketball and my academic retirement, there's more to that story. After I hung up my Chuck Taylor basketball shoes, the Naval Academy recruited this guy named David Robinson to play basketball—the same David Robinson that would become a household name. By his junior year, Robinson, or "the Admiral" as fans would call him years later, had taken Navy basketball to a level the team hadn't known in many years.

During my senior year, I watched David Robinson lead the Navy to the NCAA Division I basketball tournament—an experience that each and every kid who grew up playing basketball had dreamed about since the day they could first hit the rim. I wasn't the best player, but as I sat there and watched them play, I was torn. I couldn't have been prouder of my school, my classmates, and my former teammates, who now emerged as the Cinderella of the 1985 NCAA Tournament. But I also experienced something I'd never felt before—regret.

To this day, I doubt that I ever would have made that team—in fact, I perhaps know I wouldn't have. But I regretted listening to that academic advisor who had convinced me that I wasn't capable of getting good enough grades and playing basketball at the same time. My heart swelled with pride watching the Navy do what no other Navy basketball team had done in recent history as they defeated number-20-ranked LSU to advance to the second round of the tournament, but it also left a sour taste in my mouth. As I watched the final half of their second-round game against Maryland on TV, I promised myself that, going forward, I would never allow anyone to convince me that I was incapable of doing something. Never!

In addition to that nagging memory of regret from my time

playing basketball at the Academy, three things influenced our ultimate decision for how to move forward: One, the airlines started to hire fewer and fewer pilots in the early 1990s, and some even furloughed their more junior hires to save money.

Two, we really did love the adventure and sense of service. Not only did I enjoy the type of flying I did in the Navy, but I had also become senior enough that I'd earned my initial leadership opportunities. I wasn't liquored up in title or rank, but I did get an incredible sense of satisfaction serving in a position where I could help others. I had a passion for making a positive difference for the folks who worked for me. I had a passion for serving.

And finally, reason number three made for the dealbreaker. I was convinced that we'd never enjoy any toad in the hole parties if we ever crossed over to the airlines. Yes, that sealed the deal. Those experiences had such a positive influence on Amy and me that we both agreed to stay the course, and more importantly, to stay Navy as we rolled the dice on where that choice would take us in the years to come.

I should stress that the decision to stay Navy wasn't one I made on my own. Amy and I always made big decisions family decisions, and this one was no different. It's easy to look back now on a career that would ultimately take us to thirty-five years in uniform. During my time at the Naval Academy, those classmates in my company would have probably voted me as most unlikely to serve past the requisite five years, let alone make a decades-long career in naval aviation and achieve flag rank as a two-star admiral.

Our decision to stay Navy resulted in ten total deployments—that's over five cumulative years apart as a family.

Despite that separation, we had a family as strong as the families that both Amy and I had grown up in. We ate dinner together at the dining room table every night when I could commute home. We went to movies together. We hiked, fished, and camped together. We saw more kids' little league baseball, football, swimming, and basketball than I ever wanted to imagine. Due to the combination of separation and old-fashioned family values, we came out on top and grew stronger and stronger each year.

In addition to those ten deployments, we also did our share of moving around from one assignment to another. Not just a few times. Let's say a lot of times. In fact, we were given a gift from a friend when we first married that continues to hang on our wall today. That gift started with a small hand-painted wooden house that reads "Home Is Where the Navy Sends Us." Under that brightly painted house hang several wooden blocks that are hand-painted with specific duty station locations in the order we've served. I say several, but when we retired in July 2020, the count had grown to nineteen. Yes, in our thirty-five-year career, the Navy had sent us to nineteen different new homes. That means we had to pack up nineteen different houses, watch the movers haul our growing household, and unpack the entire house again at our new destination. With every move as our three kids grew up, they had to make new friends and start at new schools.

As we unpacked our current house upon retiring from the Navy, Amy and I both smiled when we pulled out our "Home Is Where the Navy Sends Us" display, which now seems more like a six-foot-tall monument. We smiled because we knew the Navy wasn't going to send us anywhere from here on out.

CHAPTER 6

Best Job I Ever Had

We cannot change the cards we are dealt,
just how we play the hand.

—Randy Pausch

With our decision to remain in uniform and keep serving over the alternative of making a go at the airlines, Amy and I were in "full speed ahead" mode and anxious to see what more the Navy had to offer. Of course, I remained biased to do anything and everything I could to stay in the cockpit and fly at every opportunity the Navy gave me. Having said that, I learned quickly that what I wanted to do and what the Navy wanted me to do were not always in complete harmony. I knew that, to a certain extent, I would need to play the game until I became eligible to retire at twenty years. To remain in the cockpit and continue flying in more senior ranks, I had to stay competitive along the way to earn future promotions. With each promotion, I'd find other opportunities to fly commensurate with additional responsibility within a given squadron. In other words, along with flying, I'd also have much greater leadership responsibilities associated with greater seniority and selective Navy processes. At the time, that was a secondary priority. I just wanted to fly.

My first chance to explore all those flying opportunities in front of me provided a wakeup call like having a bucket of ice thrown on you in the middle of a deep sleep. I knew heading into our assignment to fly in Canada that the Navy didn't necessarily consider that a competitive job. In Navy lingo, that means those making promotion decisions wouldn't consider it favorable when they would one day compare my record with that of my peers. Frankly, others told me it was the kiss of death. But I'd wanted to fly. I'd wanted to instruct. I'd wanted to have fun while making a difference. And that I did.

When it came time to explore my next assignment, the officer responsible for career management and assignments made a pretty direct assessment of my potential. Mind you, he didn't know me from Adam. He only based his assessment on the knowledge that I had accepted a non-career-enhancing assignment that many perceived as a fun versus meaningful pilot training production. With that in mind, I made that initial phone call and asked what flying jobs he might have available.

I became highly self-aware when he told me, "Not so much for you. You've been having fun while your peers have been working hard. You're on my list for a boat. For guys like you, beggars can't be choosers."

That made it pretty clear where I stood in that one-way conversation. But that discussion—more specifically, the prospect of going to the boat—didn't faze me. I was all in and saw that as a prerequisite path to get me back in the cockpit as soon as possible. In fact, the boat thing actually gave me one of the most meaningful leadership opportunities I'd ever had.

"Boat" is naval jargon for ship—in this case, an aircraft carrier. Odd you might say for a guy who had flown nothing but large, fixed-wing aircraft for his initial six years in the Navy, and shore based at that. The Navy doesn't think like that. Terms like "diversity of experience" and "disassociated sea tour" really serve to take one out of their element. The uninitiated are dropped in and on something as powerful and dangerous as an aircraft carrier, taking them completely out of their comfort zone. Not only are you expected to perform at an incredibly high level, but lives depend on what you do. A bit daunting for a brand-new guy on board, but if I couldn't fly, working on the flight deck of an aircraft carrier was the next best thing.

In my formal written orders to serve onboard the USS Kitty Hawk, the Navy assigned me as a catapult and arresting gear officer. In less formal terms, sailors affectionately refer to the flight deck as the "roof" and the team of catapult and arresting gear officers as the "shooters." Their role requires responsibility for the safe launch and recovery of aircraft on the flight deck. One can easily identify the shooters by their yellow flight deck jerseys when they step foot on the most dangerous four acres of real estate ever known to man.

I quickly learned that the flight deck environment was not for the faint of heart since the job called for an up close and personal experience with jets and helicopters as their engines turned and they taxied within inches of one another (and you) on their way to launch or just having recovered. At any given moment, steam rose from a catapult after a jet raced down the track for launch while another jet landed by catching a wire in what's known as a controlled crash. It was a common requirement to duck or take a knee to avoid getting run over. Everyone who worked on the flight deck had to mind their own personal safety and that of their buddies working alongside them because of the violent and dangerous working environment.

I learned as a twenty-eight-year-old junior officer up there that the hardest-working group of young men and women with whom I'd ever served surrounded me. For the most part, those young men and women who worked the flight deck had only recently joined the Navy. They had graduated from boot camp, received their initial technical training, and completed the rest of their specific trade training real time in a formal on-the-job training program tailored to their specific duties.

Think about that: Four acres of flight deck. Throw in dozens of multi-million-dollar aircraft often loaded with armament for given missions and moving about the tightly restrictive confines defined by ocean in every direction. Now think about a precision dance choreographed with every movement. More accidents should happen, but they don't due to the training and professionalism of the sailors and officers who work the deck. Many of the folks who contributed to the safe execution of that dance were under the age of twenty. I loved every minute of working in that environment. What an incredible place to call home.

That assignment onboard the USS Kitty Hawk opened my eyes to the fact that, despite my passion for flying, other things offset the lack of a cockpit and flight hours on my Navy journey. I helped lead two large divisions during my time on Kitty Hawk and was responsible for the training, welfare, and safety of hundreds of young men and women, many away from home for the very first time. These young men and women worked in harm's way in what I consider to be the most dangerous work environment known to man. Underpaid, overworked, yet fiercely loyal to the mission and fiercely loyal to serving our Navy and our country. Without a doubt, otherwise common people answering a call to do uncommon things.

What an honor for me to lead these young heroes, to sit down and listen to them, to help achieve a positive outcome for someone struggling with work, having problems with a new marriage, or overcoming a pay issue. Being in a position where I could help, often after being up for twenty hours working on the roof, helped reinforce our decision to stay Navy, where we could make a positive difference. There were only two things I missed during that tour: flying and toad in the hole parties.

Throughout my career, fortune favored me. No, I didn't fly every assignment, but unlike most others, I had ten tours during my Navy career that afforded me the opportunity to lead from the cockpit, as I like to tell my friends. Throughout that journey, we faced some difficult assignments—some more time consuming than others that took me away from home far more often than anyone wants and some that forced us to deal with various personal tragedies. But with each of those challenging circumstances along the way, I always tried to remain focused on my personal mission. I served in that squadron or on that staff in that specific moment during that specific tragedy or challenge so I could make a positive difference in leading and supporting those who worked for me.

"You are such a giver," I was told during one such hardship. "You could easily hand off what you are doing to support that person to someone else, but you choose to be involved. You choose to lead by your example." On a personal level, those opportunities when I could be a positive influence or make a difference were exactly why I continued to serve.

Yes, I had always chosen the path to fly over more career-enhancing staff tours, but I made those decisions because I genuinely had a passion for teaching and loved my time instructing hundreds upon hundreds of younger naval aviators. And during those first assignments, I deployed to every corner of the globe. I even commanded and piloted an aircraft that literally flew around the world on a visit to P-3 bases and deployment sites everywhere our aircraft and crews operated. Later in my career, the Navy selected me to command at various levels of increasing size and scope: squadron, wing, group, and joint task force. Plus, before I retired, I was entrusted with the Navy's largest shore command, where I was responsible for the preponderance of the Navy's training and education programs. Those opportunities gave me exactly what I wanted with increasing seniority and responsibility: the ability to positively influence the lives of the men and women who worked for me and the ability to effect positive changes in Navy processes and programs.

In retrospect, as a simple Navy pilot, I guess I've also had some unique opportunities that have forced me to stray off aviation's beaten path. One of those amazing paths led me toward service for two years in the White House Situation Room as the senior military representative. I was first the director of operations and then, in my final year, I was the senior director during a period of time that witnessed the Arab Spring and the Osama Bin Laden takedown. My day-to-day duties routinely took me to the Oval Office to assist with the technical phone setup for head of state phone calls between the President and his peers around the world. When someone first explained this part of the job to me, I thought, "How hard can that be? I'm sure we could train a monkey to do that!" Once again, I'd learn the hard way that I wasn't the smartest guy in the world.

It came as a complete surprise to me the day I received a call from our assignments branch, asking for an updated biography. I had just completed the National War College, where I had studied National Resource Management, spending a great deal of time learning the technical side of acquisition and logistics associated with the national industrial supply base that supports both commercial and defense aviation. My name had come up as a prospective nomination for a high-visibility position on the National Security Staff within the White House Situation Room. No doubt, it sounded like it might be too good to be true, and although I knew very little about the job itself, I was all in for the nomination.

That process took nearly three months from the time that I submitted my initial updated biography, as I worked my way through a series of in-person interviews. The job sounded more and more interesting as the process went on. They invited me to visit in person and learn more about operations within the Situation Room, a location that many people only imagine and a room that is typically shrouded in secrecy to the general public.

On my fourth visit to the West Wing, still working my way through the arduous interview and assessment process, an assistant escorted me to the West Wing lobby, where many have waited for appointments with the President, Vice President, or other high-ranking cabinet members. That day, it was just some Navy captain looking for a job. I had studied up on each of the key players on the National Security Staff who could influence my hiring. I read about their individual responsibilities within the staff and tried to reconcile how that role might impact me, or more appropriately, how I might support them one day if I was selected for the job.

When General Jim Jones, the National Security Advisor and former Commandant of the Marine Corps and Commander, U.S. European Command, entered the room, I knew exactly who he was. I had dressed in my service dress blue uniform, as was protocol for any military members attending meetings in the White House, and I took a deep breath as he approached and extended his hand in greeting.

I followed the National Security Advisor into his office, where we exchanged a few pleasantries before he cut to the chase.

"So, do you have any questions for me today, Kyle?"

I wasn't exactly comfortable but had come to learn in my previous interviews and interactions with West Wing staff that it was important to be forward and to the point.

"Yes, sir! It's an honor to be considered for the position. So, I guess at this point, I'm interested to know when you'll make a decision on who your next director of operations will be in the Situation Room."

Clearly, he'd handled much more difficult questions before. Not missing a beat, he looked toward the west window in his office. Then, he looked back to me and very matter-of-factly said, "You wouldn't be here if I hadn't already selected you. When can you start?"

With a moment of elation after hearing that good news came a sobering realization that every task, every project, and every interaction associated with the White House Situation Room demanded perfection each and every day. For the next two years I was reminded daily of the expectations and gravity of the job and its associated responsibilities.

The Situation Room sits within the first floor of the West Wing of the White House that some affectionately call the basement. Despite most people's assumption, it's much more than a single room. Supporting several mission areas, the Situation Room actually includes a group of three classified conference rooms of varying sizes, several individual offices, a watch floor, a secure video teleconferencing hub, and a communications suite that hosts several communications technicians.

The fast-paced atmosphere never lets up. Everyone who is selected for assignment to the White House Situation Room represents the best of their respective military service branch or government agency. I had the responsibility of scheduling daily sensitive conferences and enabling classified communications that ranged from phone calls to video conferencing to piecing together and reporting intelligence updates from a variety of sources and agencies for senior White House officials. We had no margin for error in an operations center that never slept.

I've heard people adamant in the belief that there's no such place for one expecting perfect performance. To those, I respond, "You've never worked in the White House Situation Room." When I worked there, I felt like a major league pitcher coming to the ballpark night after night with every expectation that I'd throw perfect game after perfect game, without fail, for two consecutive seasons. The thought of a hit batter or a base on balls was out of the question. We couldn't afford anything less than perfection.

One of our responsibilities included providing technical assistance and setup for head of state phone calls. Although most of our interaction supported calls that required a small handful of trusted agents to visit the Oval Office, there really wasn't a location in which we couldn't connect a call between the President and anyone with whom he wanted to talk. To be clear, any call between the President of the United States and any other leader of the free world was far from just a phone call. The protocols involved precise scheduling and a technical aspect that I soon became intimately familiar with.

On one call, I can remember thinking there was no way we could pull that one off—he's going to have to find another time. Wrong answer—and even a "wronger" answer, if that's a word, for the President of the United States. As I recall, the sensitive topic of this conversation required that we set up a secure encrypted call between the Oval Office and the foreign head of state. As if that wasn't hard enough, the foreign head of state was in a remote location without telephones. So, we cobbled together a plan that involved borrowing a secure phone from another U.S. government agency office nearly 100 kilometers away from the intended call site and recruiting a willing technician to set up the phone and a satellite receiver the day of the intended call. We placed several test calls to verify we had covered all our bases and waited for show time. Throughout the planning, setup, and testing, I could think only one thing: This will never work.

Fifteen minutes prior to the scheduled call, I went up to the Oval Office and waited patiently in the outer office until summoned by someone close to the President.

"Come in. He's ready."

I pulled out the phone, and after several attempts through our switchboard, the call connected. We waited for the President to nod that he was ready as he reviewed some preparatory notes. So far, so good.

I'm not going to lie—I had gotten pretty comfortable with these calls. It had become fairly routine to just go up to the Oval Office, wish the President a good morning, get dialed in, and look sharp until the call ended. I'd then put the phone back under the table and disappear just as quietly as I had entered.

Not so much on this call. For the first few minutes, I'm not sure whether I breathed. The connection scratched and crackled, but they were talking. I thought, "Maybe this won't be the catastrophe I had first imagined." Then, the call dropped.

"Sorry, Mr. President. We'll get you reconnected," I said.

Shortly, they were talking again like nothing had happened. *Whew!* Then, static. Nothing but static.

"Please let me hear something," I said, reaching for the phone.

And then, the static stopped, replaced by a dial tone.

I scrambled with the switchboard but could hear the President, our Commander in Chief and leader of the most powerful nation in the world, as he shook his head, asking, "It's just a phone call. Why is this so hard?"

It was all I could do not to give him an honest answer to make sure he understood the consecutive miracles and technical wizardry that only MacGyver could patch together.

Realizing that honesty wasn't necessarily the best option at this point, I cut my losses and told him, "We'll do better next time." I had to fight to live another day. And you know what I was thinking about the whole time? *I sure wish I were flying right now instead of standing in the Oval Office.*

Despite the "cool factor" of working in the West Wing and having the opportunity to travel with the President on Air Force One, it's like any other job, and it was common to have late nights in the office. While it was never popular on the home front, Amy always understood the unwritten code, knowing that most times I couldn't tell her the specifics of my job or why I would be late based on security classifications or sensitivity of a given issue. But it didn't take her long to realize that date night was on hold when I told her, "Honey, I won't be home on time tonight. Make sure you watch the news this evening."

Although that subtle hint about watching the news happened often during my time within the White House Situation Room, one example stands well above any of the others. It took months to unravel, but no doubt I felt like I played an unassuming role in history as a simple Navy captain performing my job within the West Wing.

It is worth emphasizing that, given the sensitive nature of the intelligence, policy deliberations, and phone conversations that we heard in our individual roles, discretion was not only expected, but any lack of discretion was grounds for immediate dismissal. And I don't mean the "you have the weekend to clear your desk" type of dismissal. More like an unexpected visit by White House security to escort you immediately to the nearest gate, take away your security badge, and bid you to never return. Ever.

On a spring morning in 2011, one of the more senior White House directors came into my office, shut the door, and asked whether he could request a favor. He had a meeting that needed to be added to the schedule that afternoon—a meeting that required the utmost discretion and secrecy. Typically, all meetings conducted within any of the Situation Room conference spaces are displayed on a schedule board, visible to anyone with access to the West Wing. For this meeting, he asked me to display the meeting time as "Blocked" as opposed to putting a specific meeting title to include attendees. To further pique my curiosity, he asked me to disable the in-room cameras. We used those for my staff to determine whether someone was still in the room, to deliver a message if needed, or to pull someone out for an important call.

"Yes, sir. Got it."

He also directed me that under no circumstances should anyone other than the senior director or myself enter the room during the meeting to pass any messages.

"No problem, sir."

Finally, he asked me to help three people from the CIA who would attend the meeting gain access to the largest of the three conference rooms and to set up a specific model for use in the afternoon briefing.

A motto I shared with every new employee selected to serve in the Situation Room was, "There are a lot of important people in the West Wing. We are not them." So, I obliged and set to work making certain that the meeting went off without a hitch. Given the closed door and specific directions, it didn't take a rocket scientist to figure out that this was a big deal. I just didn't know how big of a deal.

I did everything asked of me, and about thirty minutes prior to the scheduled blocked time, I met the three young analysts from the CIA, who brought with them what appeared to be a large plywood box, several inches thick and broad in dimension. Given our close interaction with all the Secret Service agents who stood security detail outside the main entrance to the Situation Room, it was an easy task to help the young analysts gain access, even with the unusually large "prop" they brought to the meeting.

Once inside the room, they asked where to set up their model. Given the fact that the President always sat at the head of the table, surrounded by his advisors in rank of seniority, I told them it was probably best to set it up at the far end of the table. That could certainly change, and the model could be moved during the course of the meeting if needed.

When they opened the box, it lay flat on the table and was obviously a scale replica of some housing compound. It wasn't anything fancy but clearly depicted a fenced compound with various inner buildings and living quarters. It reminded me of the many compounds that I'd seen before from 25,000 feet or so, flying reconnaissance missions over Afghanistan or Iraq, but it was unidentifiable to me as to a specific location. And that was it.

We hosted a series of similar follow-up meetings over the next several weeks with the same requirements for the setup. No cameras, no meeting title displayed, and assistance as required for any "special visitors and props." I remained in the dark regarding the specific goal or outcome of these meetings but knew that something big was being discussed. I couldn't let my curiosity distract me given the multitude of daily tasks we had to complete without error. On occasion, I had to pass a note to someone in the closed briefing, and every time, the model of that nondescript compound stayed clearly front and center of whatever discussions occurred behind those tightly closed doors. Yes, something big. Something bold. But I still lacked any specific context to realize the history happening in those meetings.

After a series of those meetings, we had another visitor, Brigadier General Brad Webb, who served as the number two behind Vice Admiral Bill McRaven, Commander of the Joint Special Operations Command. After a courtesy introduction,

I helped him set up his gear so that he could establish whatever communications network connections that he deemed necessary.

Fortunately, I had one of the very best communications experts in the field leading our secure communications team. This guy was the MacGyver of the White House. He had served under several previous administrations, and I was convinced he could turn a lump of charcoal, duct tape, and a D-cell battery into a secure phone that was capable of underwater transmission and doubled as a laser gun. He was the best of the best.

Within days, Brigadier General Webb agreed that, through a series of communications checks with the other end, he had what he needed. At the end of one long afternoon, he came into my office to say thanks and confirmed what I had come to know—that we had a world-class communications team. On that afternoon, he mentioned something about a mission to capture Osama Bin Laden. Now the puzzle pieces became clear. Historic! We planned to capture the world's most wanted terrorist, and that planning had occurred right under my nose.

It's fair to say that the rest is, quite literally, history. The raid went off with a highly skilled complement of special operators that executed in an immensely professional manner. As the mission unfurled, the connectivity that our team painstakingly set up in the Situation Room's smallest conference room allowed near real-time awareness for the President and his senior policy team. Yes, it's probably the most famous image ever released from within the White House Situation Room. Trust me, the photographic image of that moment captures only a small part of that historic event.

Years later, after attaining flag officer rank and my first star, a major turning point for any military career, the Navy selected me to run the Joint Task Force at Guantanamo Bay, Cuba. As a career aviator, I lived to fly and loved to instruct. What did I know about prison operations, the legal intricacies of day-to-day operations, or the political visibility that laced the world's most recognizable detention facility? The short answer is that I knew absolutely nothing.

When I landed at the Windward airfield in Guantanamo Bay just two days before assuming command, that feeling of "What have you gotten yourself into?" overcame me. But as with everything else I'd learned in my career, the more senior you become, the more you are required to focus on the strategic nature of a mission and not the nuts and bolts of every intricate aspect of the broader mission. Equally important, the more senior you become, the more you are expected to simply lead your people through any variety of circumstances they might encounter in executing the mission that you've been given.

At GTMO, our command mission focus required us to provide safe and humane conditions for the appointed detainees held under my charge. More importantly, the military tasked me with leading 2,200 young American servicemen and -women from the Army, Navy, Air Force, Marines, and Coast Guard as we conducted our mission in a way that demonstrated to the world a professionalism and capability for what many considered a controversial mission.

During that tour, we often took advantage of an outdoor theater where new movie releases filled the screen every night of the week. My senior enlisted leader was an amazing man with endless energy and limitless enthusiasm. He was a poster child for professionalism and fitness and grew up as a "tanker." For many years, my sergeant major served in Marine Corps armored tank units and never shied away from sharing stories about his good old days. So, it wasn't a surprise to me when he stopped by my house one night while Amy was off island visiting family. With an enthusiastic gleam in his eye, he said "Let's go, sir. I'm taking you to the movies."

That night, at the Downtown Lyceum, we watched the movie *Fury*. The film tells the story of a U.S. tank crew fighting in Nazi Germany during the final weeks of the European theater during World War II.

The movie focuses on one specific tank crew led by a grizzled sergeant and consisting of a hodgepodge of soldiers fighting for their lives as the Nazis fought like trapped wild animals looking to escape from a corner. As the other tanks in their platoon are destroyed by a much superior German tank division, the crew of "Fury" receives orders to capture and hold a crossroads to protect the division's rear. Upon arriving at the crossroads, a landmine damages their tank, rendering it immobile and a veritable sitting duck for advancing German troops. When the crew detects a Waffen-SS battalion approaching their position with a clear intent on taking control of that critical crossroad, their tank commander tells his younger crew to get away.

"Go save yourselves and live another day to fight." Having said that, he climbs back into the crippled tank "Fury" and prepares to engage the advancing enemy.

Having witnessed their sergeant's commitment to complete their assigned mission, one by one, each member of the crew joins him, knowing full well they face certain death in a fight they know they can't win. Ultimately, the rest of the crew decides to stay and confront the enemy and, fully understanding their fate, prepares for their impending fight.

As they reminisce about all they'd accomplished as a tank crew, the sergeant breaks out a hidden bottle of liquor from his rucksack, passing it around for each of the crew to share. As they pass the bottle, the viewer hears the sergeant whisper to himself, "Best job I ever had." He then closes his eyes, in all likelihood thinking about much better times and how proud he is of his crew.

In unison, each of the other four crew members acknowledge their leader's whispers, and while they understand the likely outcome of an overmatched fight, they too echo those words: "Best job I ever had."

During my remaining time in GTMO, I often thought about that movie, and more specifically, that specific choice of words. Faced with certain death, the crew reaffirmed their commitment to their mission. More importantly, as they whispered those final words, they reaffirmed, under the worst of conditions and circumstances, their commitment to each other.

Detention operations in GTMO was an unforgiving mission. Our U.S. forces serving there do so with the utmost professionalism. Despite that professionalism, the media routinely misinforms the public about how we conducted that mission. As if misinformation from many media outlets isn't enough, detainees often subject their guards and medical support personnel to abusive language, threaten them with physical violence, and attempt to assault them with mixed "cocktails" of unimaginable bodily fluids that they try to throw or squirt on any U.S. serviceman or -woman who comes close enough to contact.

"Best job I ever had." During my year as the joint task force commander, those same servicemen and -women never—I repeat, never—lost their composure or compromised their professionalism with any sort of retaliation. Shortly after assuming command, I implemented accountability measures that all but stopped many of these abuses from detainees targeted at my troops. Frankly, I never had to carry out any of the accountability measures. As soon as word spread through the detention cells what consequences were in store for unacceptable behavior toward my troops, things changed for the better.

Yes, we had a tough mission. Yes, we had a politically charged mission. Yes, the media often mischaracterized our mission to the general public. Despite all of that, working with those exceptional men and women—another example of otherwise common people committed to doing uncommon things—was truly the best job I ever had.

In my last flying job while on active duty, I commanded the Navy's entire Maritime Patrol and Reconnaissance Group, a big title that boils down to a responsibility for four airwings, fifteen squadrons, and over 7,500 individuals who supported, fixed, and flew our nearly 150 aircraft. Needless to say, I loved it. I especially loved the opportunity to get out of my office and visit both flight lines at our homeports as well as those forward deployed around the globe. My perspective about taking care of people and leveraging my position to make sure that we took care of our servicemen and -women, the civilian employees who were equally critical to our mission, and our families hadn't changed since I had first commanded a 400-person squadron nearly a decade prior. But my appreciation for the service, sacrifice, and hard work they invested in our mission grew each and every day I was blessed to serve with them.

Every time I had a chance to pop in unexpectedly to an office or a flight line work center or to go flying with one of our aircrews, it gave me a chance to recenter my efforts on our people. *What's your name? Where are you from? Tell me about yourself. What do you like most about what you do? What can I do to help you?* Our people, including their families, were tough and resilient. I often talked about them as heroes and believe that with every fiber of my being.

When I was a kid, back in my gym rat days, I had a much different perspective. Back then, if you asked me who my heroes were, I'd quickly single out professional athletes. I wasn't a big Hollywood guy, so actors and popular singers never crossed my mind as they typically do with kids today. I don't think I was unusual in that regard since public heroes are typically very recognizable through the media, movies, and other accessible venues.

That perspective changed significantly as I matured in uniform and better understood the concept of service and serving a cause bigger than oneself. Yes, you could say that a common link exists between the heroes I worshiped in high school and those I respect today in that they both wear uniforms. But those heroes I respect today are the men and women who serve. They serve as members of the Armed Forces. They serve as medical professionals and as first responders. They don't do what they do for money. They do what they do to help others. They do it to make a difference in their community, in their service or field, and in our country. My heroes fit a mold cast from otherwise common people committed to doing uncommon things. That's why every day in uniform for me, almost thirty-six years, was absolutely the best job I ever had.

CHAPTER 7

Life's "Fatal Encounter"

The catastrophe that awaits everyone from a single false move,
wrong turn, fatal encounter. Every life has such a moment.
What distinguishes us is whether—and how—we ever come back.

—Charles Krauthammer

For years, I watched Mr. Charles Krauthammer on Fox News and enjoyed his conservative and sometimes outspoken political perspective. But until he passed away in 2018, I never realized that he was wheelchair bound. While a student at Harvard, Krauthammer had experienced a diving accident that had rendered him permanently paralyzed. Now made aware of his circumstances, I could tell that his injury and paralysis didn't get in the way of any of his personal or professional success. After his hospitalization, he went on to earn his board certification in psychiatry, contributed to planning in psychiatric research during the Carter administration, and eventually won a Pulitzer Prize for his work on The Washington Post.

Looking back, Friday, March 16, 2018, began like many other days that I'd experienced since assuming command of the

Naval Education and Training Command some seven months earlier. I had scheduled a busy combination of meetings, program updates, and telephone calls to wrap up the week and prepare for the next. With family in town, I looked forward to a relaxing weekend that would take us to the beach, local restaurants, and, since my grandson was with us, a trip to the National Naval Aviation Museum just down the street from our quarters. That was the plan. But a wise man once said, "Life tends to get a vote." For me, life would take a drastic turn that night and would alter my physical abilities as well as my appreciation for things that I'd previously taken for granted.

As we prepared to turn in for the evening, I suffered a freak accident. Everyone else had gone to bed after we had watched a movie, and then I headed up for the night. We lived in a historic home known as Quarters A at the Pensacola Naval Air Station. Although it had all the modern conveniences, it had several more sets of stairs than modern homes. To the best of my recollection, I had a simple "slip and fall" from a staircase that led to our living floor in the house that put me flat on my back. I lay there, unable to move my lower half and calling for help.

The difference with this fall was what my neurosurgeon can only describe as the one-in-a-million way I landed on my back. Days later, he would describe the damage done to my vertebrae as something he'd only seen before in significant high-speed car accidents. Unfortunately, he also noted that the damage appeared much, much worse than he'd originally imagined based off the pre-surgery MRI results.

As luck would have it, the end result from a high-speed car crash was the same for me. Although my memories of that night remain blurred, I clearly remember the excruciating pain like I'd never felt before as the EMS crew loaded me onto the gurney and we sped off in the ambulance. Due to the pain, I went in and out of consciousness that night. I can barely remember the fall and only have slight recollections of the events leading up to my surgery nearly twelve hours later—a surgery that lasted over six hours and resulted in two titanium rods, multiple screws, and a large vertical incision that took thirty-five staples to close. To this day, I still don't have a clear recollection of the fall or what put me on my back that fateful night.

As I became lucid after the surgery, I began to realize the impact of what had happened. Although painkillers somewhat masked the pain, I started to understand that the trauma of my fall had resulted in shattered vertebrae and damage to my spinal cord. As the surgeon explained it to me, I was fortunate because, in medical terms, he considered mine an "incomplete" injury. That means I'd have some feeling, even if faint, since my spinal cord hadn't been completely severed. A complete injury means that all messages between the brain and spinal cord are lost. Despite the shattered bone fragments in my back, thankfully, my spinal cord had remained intact. That was the good news. The impact from my fall, however, had caused enough swelling and trauma that it left me without feeling. As I became more and more aware, I soon realized that I had lost nearly all the feeling below my waist.

For the first time since my surgery, I wrestled with the reality that I might live some portion of my life as the victim of some level of paralysis. At the same time that I was coming to terms with what my injury really meant, the surgeon had given Amy a grim outlook after completing my surgery. The guy wore a Daffy Duck tie because he mainly worked as a pediatric neurosurgeon, but I'm fortunate that I had the flat-out best surgeon in the state for this specific injury.

"Mrs. Cozad, the damage was more significant than we could see on the MRI earlier today before the surgery. It's likely, due to the damage I was required to repair, that there will be a permanent level of paralysis for your husband. I'd speculate that your husband will be confined to a wheelchair for the rest of his life."

Wow! Talk about unexpected news. Neither Amy nor I were remotely prepared for thinking about the likely future that my surgeon had predicted. As we both talked for the first time after the surgery, neither one of us wanted to tell the other what we knew. Amy understood, conceptually, the bleak prognosis the doctor had shared immediately following the surgery. At the same time, I knew for a fact that I had lost feeling in my legs.

I wrestled with the first question someone in my situation typically asks after a catastrophic injury. It's human nature. *Why me?* Why did this happen to me? I am a father, husband, and granddad. I have so much that I need to do and so much left to accomplish. I am also a successful flag officer, commanding the Navy's largest shore command. This didn't seem fair. It shouldn't have happened to me. Things like this always seem to happen to other people, don't they?

Since my accident, I've had plenty of time to talk to a variety of doctors, physical and occupational therapists, nurses, and well-intentioned people with many different opinions on the subject of post-accident psychology. Most of those people with experience on the issue will tell you that it's rather common to feel guilt, or even self-pity, when a bad prognosis resulting from a traumatic accident is first understood. I was no different.

There I lay in my hospital bed, unable to move, for an entire eight days following my surgery. Flat on my back, the pain hard to imagine, as well-meaning ICU nurses prodded and poked me at all hours of the day and night. This was not the way I had intended to spend the weekend with my family.

Why me? More human nature here. I was a provider. It was my role to care for Amy and for my kids. How could I do that from a wheelchair? My mind next raced toward thoughts of a near-term medical retirement. In retrospect, I realize that the painkillers provided some extra incentive for these thoughts, but I could think of little else than those unknowns. I wondered where I could order a minivan with wheelchair access. I reached for my iPhone to Google how much a two-star admiral would make in retirement with a full disability compensation. I really felt like the news I had just received had snapped life as I knew it from my fingers at the peak of my career. I had plenty of time in the hospital to think about unfinished projects around the house, about trips we had scheduled over the summer, and about life that I still intended to live with my extended family.

I received several texts and phone calls inquiring how I was doing, but with plenty of time in a hospital room, in between painkillers, I spent every passing day consumed with thoughts about what this injury really meant for my future. Our future, really, because what this meant for my wife, kids, and grandson concerned me just as much as my concerns over myself.

Why me? The thoughts randomly entered my mind. There were plenty of people who weren't as high performing as I considered myself to be. Plenty of other folks who didn't care about other people like I do. Plenty of others who could have taken my place. It was during that short "Why me?" phase during the initial days following my surgery when Amy first brought me a page from something she had read the night before. I read that Charles Krauthammer quote over and over to myself: "The catastrophe that awaits everyone from a single false move, wrong turn, fatal encounter. Every life has such a moment. What distinguishes us is whether—and how—we ever come back."

Krauthammer's quote instantly became personal and stayed with me during my time in the ICU. It provided a powerful image of the possibilities that lay before me as opposed to anything I might have lost. It was as if he spoke directly to me. In the scariest moment of my entire life, Krauthammer brought me an escape. How would I come back? I took his message as a personal challenge and realized that I had a decision to make. I could let my accident define an uncertain future. I could allow my accident to take away everything I had worked so hard to achieve. I could let it define who I would become and lay in bed feeling sorry for myself. Or I could do something with my situation and tackle this injury head on.

I felt as if some person who had suffered a similar injury many years ago had personally challenged me, and that person had made an incredible comeback and risen to achieve some pretty significant personal and professional accomplishments. Would I choose to come back? How would I come back? My Type A personality and years of learning about how to respond to an emergency in the aircraft kicked into gear. How did I respond to my academic performance challenges at the Naval Academy? How did I respond to that severely sprained ankle before high school basketball tryouts? I'd never walked away from a challenge up to this point in my life, and I wasn't about to start now. I wasn't sure how I'd do it or how far I could take any sort of recovery, but I knew one thing for certain: I couldn't simply "walk it off" this time, like my dad had told me to do with that sprained ankle.

CHAPTER 8

Relentless Positivity

What is the difference between an obstacle and an opportunity?
Our attitude toward it. Every opportunity has a difficulty,
and every difficulty has an opportunity.

—J. Sidlow Baxter

In addition to that Krauthammer quote that I kept thinking about, another relatively simple and innocent question really served to push me beyond my "Why me?" stage of recovery. That simple question takes me back to my initial days in the hospital when my ICU nurse took the opportunity to summarize the list of the medications that I had been prescribed following my surgery. She explained the importance for each patient to know and understand each one of their prescribed medications as part of the recovery process. Fair enough. As you can probably imagine, doctors prescribed me painkillers, blood thinners, and anti-inflammatory pills. That all made sense to me, but one pill really struck me as odd. The nurse told me that I had also been prescribed an antidepressant.

That one caught my attention. "Ma'am, I broke my back.

What does an antidepressant do for me?"

She paused for a second and offered the explanation and question that just about put me on the floor. "Well, typically after a serious life-changing injury like yours, it's not uncommon for patients to become severely depressed and even have thoughts of self-harm. Have you been depressed or thought about hurting yourself since your accident?"

Another wow moment. I wasn't sure if I should be offended or if she was even serious. After a long, uncomfortable pause, I almost laughed at her. "Do you happen to know what I do for a living?"

I am blessed to be a father of three awesome young adults. I have an incredible grandson who adores his Poppa. After decades together, I find myself more and more in love with my wife each and every day we're together. And I'm a naval officer, trusted to command the Navy's largest shore command and to impact the lives of thousands of sons and daughters who have chosen to serve. I understood the medical staff saw a patient in the hospital with a serious, potentially life-changing injury, but despite those odds, I still considered myself the luckiest guy in the world.

I wasn't exactly thrilled about being in the hospital pondering what life held for me next, but I loved life and everything it previously held and everything that it potentially held in the future. With that odd question, I can emphatically say that's where anything resembling a "Why me?" stage ended. It didn't take more than a few days before that thought departed my mind forever. More importantly, it allowed me—or maybe more appropriately, forced me—to focus on how soon I'd bounce back and relearn how to walk. In sports terms, it was game on!

The combination of that well-meaning question and that Krauthammer quote, "What distinguishes us is whether—and how—we ever come back," challenged me with an energy and an attitude that I can't accurately explain. I committed myself to knowing that I wouldn't allow this injury to define me. God has a plan for everything that happens in our lives, and yes, he'd handed me a doozey. I didn't understand why, but now I knew in my heart that I was here for a reason. I sure hoped for only a temporary situation, but regardless, God had a plan for me, and I was ready to carry out that plan, even though I had no idea what that entailed. It was time for me, still in the ICU, to get to work and start defining how I would come back. I love the Bible verse found in Isaiah 40, as it's always had a special meaning for me since my father's death: "…but they who wait for the Lord shall renew their strength; they shall mount up with wings like eagles; they shall run and not be weary; they shall walk and not faint." It was time for me to mount up!

Frankly, that nurse's question was also the onset of what one friend calls my "relentless positivity." I thought about that question and responded in my mind with an emphatic, "Absolutely not!" and in saying that realized I was experiencing quite the opposite of depression or thoughts of self-harm. Despite breaking my back and now facing the uncertainty of never walking again, I did consider myself perhaps the luckiest guy alive. Ironic? Yes. I knew that I was in the hospital and I had little to no feeling below my waist, but I was alive and had no doubts about how much love and support I had to carry me through this. That moment helped me define my optimism, commit to a positive attitude toward my recovery, and look forward to the full life in front of me.

For the next few days, still in pain from the surgery and as uncomfortable with my physical restrictions as I've ever been in my life, I measured the minutes and seconds until my doctor released me from my initial hospital stay. It was time for me to get to work and prove my surgeon wrong as I set out to relearn how to walk.

CHAPTER 9

Decisions, Decisions

Out of the mountain of despair, a stone of hope.
—Dr. Martin Luther King

While in the intensive care unit, Amy and I faced a difficult decision in selecting the inpatient care facility where we would spend the next several weeks and begin our road to recovery. We had no idea what to expect or what recovery even looked like, so when my primary hospital caseworker first started the conversation of rehabilitation, we really had no perspective on which to base our decision. My neurosurgeon had made it clear in his initial diagnosis telling Amy that I would likely remain wheelchair bound for the rest of my life. At that time, we didn't understand the option of rehabilitation.

Fortunately, we had the best insurance we could have asked for, and we had our choice of world-class impatient rehabilitation facilities in large metropolitan areas around the southeastern United States. In addition to those large care centers, we also had a local option. We found a rehabilitation center specializing in brain and spinal recovery within forty-five minutes of our home in our present duty station in Pensacola, Florida. Like many decisions we'd face in the coming months, we had no formal training or previous experiences on which to base our choices. Like many other people we've met and come to know on this journey, we didn't even know what questions to ask in order to make an informed decision.

Complicating matters, this discussion and decision came at a time when the medications from my post-operative pain management regimen heavily influenced my thinking. Like many other times in my life, I must admit that I probably didn't help much. Several days after the surgery, I still had a tough time comprehending what had happened and why everyone insisted on waking me up every time I closed my eyes to give me another round of pills or take my blood pressure. I could barely wrap my arms around what our life together held for us. Like so many other times in our marriage, I witnessed firsthand the uncommon strength in my wife.

I sometimes have to pinch myself to make sure I'm not dreaming when thinking of the young lady I met at the Naval Academy and later married. I remember telling a friend the night I met her, actually on my birthday, that I saw something special in her—something I'd never really felt with a girl. After she gave me her phone number at my request during that initial meeting, I told my buddy that I typically lacked the courage to call a girl after just meeting her. Not this time. I planned to follow up and call her as soon as I got back to my room. I returned to the Academy, but we didn't have phones in our rooms. Back in the day, we relied on these historic artifacts called telephone booths. So, I built up the nerve to walk to the phone booth room, and I made the call. Clearly, my intuition was on point because, in less than a year, we stood man and woman in the splendor and glory of the United States Naval Academy Chapel, where Amy found herself among the unofficial ranks of thousands of other Navy wives.

When it comes to Navy spouses, someone could actually write a multiple-volume novel in describing the unique lifestyle, personal challenges, and hardships they face. Those challenges serve to shape the incredibly tough people that many of them really didn't know they could become. The single factor that helps shape that independence and toughness more than any other is through the nature of how we operate as a naval force—that is, deployments. Every twelve to twenty-four months, sailors are called to sail, float, or fly away for various periods of time—typically multiple consecutive months at a time. My first deployment to Keflavik, Iceland, shaped what I've come to know as the most independent, toughest girl I've ever met. Eight months pregnant with our first daughter, Amy had to reconcile that her mission remained at home while I served another far away.

Her ability to handle the mission at home has never wavered. During my stay in the ICU, Amy would spend all day with me in the hospital, then drive forty-five minutes to our home on Naval Air Station Pensacola, where her first duty required tending to our two yellow Labradors. She had them both convinced through regular walks and extra treats that everything remained both normal and good. After catching up with dishes, laundry, and her everyday household chores, she'd retire to catch a few precious hours of sleep before she'd wake up, feed the dogs, and walk them one more time before heading back to the hospital for the day.

She'd also do all kinds of detailed research on a range of topics now front and center in her life. She researched the medical intricacies of paralysis. She researched back injuries. She researched different recovery programs. And before she dozed off for those few precious hours of sleep, she'd research each of the rehabilitation centers that my doctors had recommended. It took only a few short days before she developed an expertise at making phone calls to ask the right questions about various treatment regimens, availability of medical equipment, and patient-to-therapist ratios. We didn't simply want to go through the motions of rehab; we planned to own it. She seemed to know everything the doctors knew about patient care, facilities' professional reputations, success stories, and what support resources were available to visiting families.

As we talked about our options, two important factors played into our decision: prayer and family. At the end of the day, we agreed that I would be best off in the location that would best support Amy's participation in my treatment. After thirty-three years of marriage, going through something as difficult as post-accident recovery really seemed to point to one thing: We needed to be together, and unless that togetherness would negatively impact my therapy, we'd place that at the top of our decision-making criteria. And we prayed. We prayed often—possibly more so than either of us had ever done.

Having said that, we've always been faithful people. I grew up in the Methodist Church with a family that ate dinner together every evening with "Ozzie and Harriet." Like many, our faith has ebbed and flowed at times. As they say, "Life gets in the way." But we both acknowledged the fact that my accident had occurred for a reason. Neither of us understood why, but we did both understand that we needed to tackle this as a team with our faith as the most important component of our togetherness. So, after Amy's detailed research and some exhaustive prayer, we decided to stay local and trust in the West Florida Rehabilitation Institute.

I'll be honest, everyone has an opinion. Yes, everyone. There were folks who questioned our decision for my inpatient treatment, asking the same questions: Why would you opt for a smaller facility when you could go somewhere larger? Or choose something more modern? Or go with a more recognizable name?

At the end of the day, Amy's research clearly showed similarities in each of the facilities, but only one really allowed me to be with Amy. (She hasn't admitted this, but I suppose our two yellow Labradors factored into this decision as well). Only the West Florida facility kept us with the Navy family we had come to know and love during our initial time in Pensacola—an important factor for us. Having never gone through an intensive care regimen like we were about to begin, our prayers steered us toward family—our immediate family and our Navy family who had been there at every step of our career for the previous three decades. We both knew that erring on the side of family would serve us well. It had never failed us before.

CHAPTER 10

Everyone Hates Hospitals, Right?

We'd been assured it wouldn't be painful, though I might experience "discomfort," a term beloved of the medical profession that seems to be a synonym for agony that isn't yours.

—Lionel Shriver, We Need to Talk About Kevin

Frankly, I think hospitals generally earn a bad rap. Everyone, or nearly everyone, associates hospitals and the various health care professionals connected with hospitals with negative experiences. Nobody likes going to see the dentist, right? Hospitals have the same bad rap. While I can certainly sympathize with that generalization, I'll offer an alternative opinion that I formed during my thirty-three-day inpatient hospital stay at West Florida Rehabilitation Center.

To help facilitate an understanding of my opinion, I'll share a general life philosophy that applies to everything I do. I'm a firm believer that, regardless of your line of work, many contributing factors bear on your potential for success. While some of those factors fall within our control, others do not. But one thing we can always control is how we manage and cultivate personal relationships and interact with the people in our lives. The way a person creates personal relationships with peers, customers, and even competitors directly impacts their potential for success. Since hospitals are living, breathing institutions that are operated for people and run by other people, personal relationships and human interaction between patients and their health care teams are no less important than in the business world.

During my stay at West Florida, I created a variety of vivid memories that influence how I now think about hospitals. I remember the exhausting therapy and exercise schedule that always led to my uncanny ability to sleep on demand—anywhere, anytime. I would sleep as soon as I lay down in bed, which had never been an issue for me. But I could also sleep in any chair and in any position. On more than one occasion, I'll freely admit that I nodded off during my therapy exercises.

I also have what I'll call less-than-fond memories of a special device I wore for the first three months of my recovery. Therapists required me to wear a specially fitted fiberglass shell designed to keep my spinal column and spinal cord immobile while they healed. Although I didn't have to wear it while lying down in bed, they required I don my "turtle shell" before getting out of bed. It served its function and helped maintain proper alignment as my spinal column healed, but it made me hot and indescribably uncomfortable.

Early during my stay in the ICU—actually, within days of receiving my fitted shell shortly after my surgery—one of the hospital technicians put it on incorrectly as they carted me off for some post-operative x-rays. Think about wearing your pants backwards. Now think of wearing your pants backwards with sandpaper scraping your body. Imagine this aggravating shell now put on backwards. It caused excruciating pain and some local bleeding since it rubbed on my surgical staples.

Well, it only happened once before I took matters into my own hands. I took charge, and from that point forward, I directed anyone and everyone who had the duty of helping me get armored up. I also allowed my son and his girlfriend to decorate the plain white shell for effect. On the front, the new design included multiple stickers of aviation squadron patches and aircraft likenesses, topped off with a vibrant "Don't Tread on Me" American flag. On the back, they placed an obnoxious red, white, and blue frog waving his frog arm in a recognizable peace sign.

Whenever anyone would approach me with the shell with the intent to help me put it on, I'd interrupt with very clear directions: "The frog goes in back, and make sure his peace sign is pointed up." After that, I never had an issue with how the shell went on.

I also recall how quickly I grew to detest anything and everything that appeared in my hospital room on the meal tray. At first, I tried to power through each meal, but that didn't last long. It didn't matter what they served. For some reason, if it appeared on the meal tray and had the warming cover over the top, it would taste terrible despite the fact that I've never been a picky eater. To this day, the thought of powdered scrambled eggs and mystery meat sausage makes my stomach turn. But the food selection wasn't the only memory I'd prefer to forget. I also hated the daily schedule, which typically started at 5:00

a.m. with my first nurse's visit to collect my vital signs. I even had my bouts of impatience if my pain medicine came too late. And to this day, I can't stand the hospital smell. But those memories fade quickly when compared to the lasting relationships I created during my stay.

Now you might consider this ironic, especially when most people generally think about hospitals in a negative way, but my inpatient stay at West Florida resulted in tremendous respect for what my entire medical team did for me. Having said that, I'll be the first to admit that not all medical staffers, whether nurses, doctors, medical technicians, or staff therapists, are created equal. But I'll also be equally honest and go on record as saying there are some absolute superstars who go well above what they are expected to do for their patients at every hospital.

West Florida Rehabilitation Center was no different. I found individuals there who stood out above the others and made an impression that I will never forget. These people went out of their way to stop in and say hello. They didn't just go through the motions to ask how I felt. They really cared, and I knew they were asking because they wanted to help. In any circumstance, these folks made it a point to connect with their patients and get to know them on a personal basis. I consider them the top 1 percent of their profession. For those unlikely and sometimes unexpected relationships that I formed in one short month, I'm forever thankful.

Before my injury, I had never spent a day in the hospital other than to visit my father before he passed away. Because of that, I only based my opinions on what I'd seen and heard from other people's experiences. With my hospitalization, however, I formed my own opinions through personal experiences that helped to disprove many of those stereotypes. The relationships I created during those relatively short thirty-three days resulted in an incredible professional respect for my caregivers, as well as created personal friendships that I know will last a lifetime. They helped nurse me back from a point where I could do almost nothing to a place where I could return home and resume a semi-normal life. How could I describe those relationships as anything short of incredible?

Like most people, Amy and I hadn't really thought or cared too much about insurance—that is, until we needed it. One great epiphany I've come to realize as a result of my injury is that the military health care system and the insurance coverage we are provided is second to none. Given the life change that a traumatic injury brings upon a family, I can't imagine having to worry about paying for what I can only assume were astronomical hospital bills associated with neurosurgery, intensive care, and then follow-on inpatient rehabilitation. As impressive as the insurance coverage that the military provides every serviceman and -woman is, an amazing, supporting team works behind the scenes. Until we really needed them, Amy and I had no idea what those excellent hospital caseworkers really did for people.

In and out of the hospital, a small group of various hospital and civilian caseworkers had the responsibility of coordinating the mundane administrative aspects of hospitalization. They tirelessly worked on behalf of their assigned patients and ensured that Amy and I didn't have to worry about insurance paperwork or ordering the various articles of medical support equipment that we'd need when we made the transition back home. More times than not, they coordinated the various administrative approvals, doctors' referrals, and insurance paperwork that never even rose to our attention. Those caseworkers were absolute professionals in every respect—so much so that I often think of them as the unsung heroes of our hospital experience.

One of the other aspects of my rehabilitation stay that really stands out was that I was able to blend in and be just another patient. I know that sounds odd, but I found it important that they treated me just like everyone else. My job didn't matter. My rank was immaterial. They didn't view me as a senior naval officer or a two-star admiral—only a patient facing similar medical conditions as the other patients there with me, regardless of where they came from. Fortunately, many of my caregivers, far removed from the military, remained completely unaware of what I did for my day job. That anonymity allowed me to really create the relationships that became so important, not only among the staff but also within my patient peer group.

As thankful as we were for the support we received from the dedicated medical staff, they couldn't provide everything for their patients. Unless one goes through a similar recovery—and I mean going through it personally—I really think it's hard to understand the psychological and physical challenges that I wrestled with every day. There is a "been there, done that"—or, in some cases, "been there, doing that"—component to really understanding the complexity of a recovery like the one I faced.

I'll acknowledge that doctors or other skilled specialists undergo years of training to master the complexities of biology, physiology, and surgical procedure. Fortunately, I had a top-notch medical team that provided me with a perfect surgery, and my follow-up care rivaled the best in class. However, typically, none of these specialists have ever felt the pain I felt. They certainly haven't felt the indescribable loss of feeling and sensation in their legs. So, there are only a handful of other people who could really understand my experience. The other patients going through similar recoveries provided their own unique perspective and sense of "I know what you're going through" that served as both a comfort and, at the same time, an incredible sense of encouragement.

At West Florida, I met other patients in treatment for paralysis similar to mine but also many patients being treated for other dissimilar injuries. Every day, regardless of the nature of a person's injury, we all watched each other. Since we all came from different social, economic, and cultural backgrounds, I found this fascinating. For most of us, had it not been for our injuries, we'd never have met. But we had something in common—going through the greatest challenge that any of us had faced in our individual lives. Because of that common challenge, we developed a unique and often nonverbal form of encouragement for one another. We became quite skilled in reading each other's body language, so we knew when someone had struggled that day and needed something as simple as a wink, a head nod, or a thumbs up to provide the encouraging support to keep going. I found it funny that we didn't always know each other's names, but from our common experience on the rehabilitation floor, we came to know one another in ways that are hard to describe.

It's difficult for me to explain the psychological aspects of having to be lifted out of bed because you no longer possess the feeling or the strength to do so on your own. Similarly, it's hard to describe how tough it is to take a step backwards and regress from a previous level of performance or a skill that you seemed to have mastered only a week prior. I think that's especially true when you are used to being a highly functional and successful individual. But in that small hospital peer group, only bonded by common rehabilitation experiences, we all learned together how to practice patience and to accept the small improvements, and more importantly, the inevitable setbacks. We all learned humility by watching each other and discovered how to embrace even the smallest of accomplishments in our long and typically difficult paths to recovery. Through those observations, we all learned the importance of trusting others and acknowledging that not only could we find acceptance in that unconditionally but that it's essential to lean on someone other than yourself for support.

Consider the following: Before my accident, the Navy trusted me with the largest shore command in the United States Navy. I had over 50,000 military, civilian, and contract employees working for me. I worked independently and wasn't afraid to make hard decisions that would impact the way our Navy trains or that would impact thousands of persons. Although I fully understand the value of individual contributions to our complex recruiting, training, and education mission, I preferred self-sufficiency in my profession.

After my accident, in addition to learning patience and recognizing that a full recovery isn't a short-term effort, I also quickly realized that I couldn't do this on my own. In the hospital, some patients learned this the hard way, but I realized early on what an incredible support network I had cheering on my recovery. Amy sat at the top of that list. While she provided my spiritual support, we also had an incredible network of community, staff, and big Navy supporters eager to do anything we might ask. They were all complemented by an amazing occupational and physical therapy team that was totally committed to taking me as far as physically possible in my recovery and rehabilitation.

Unconditional trust is something that didn't come easy for me, but I quickly realized that, like a small child learning to crawl or walk, I needed to do something I wasn't used to doing. I needed to rely on my support network.

By watching other patients in the ward on the therapy floor with a week or two more experience than me, this otherwise highly independent naval officer quickly changed his entire outlook. I didn't have to do this on my own. Frankly, I couldn't do it on my own. So, I learned how to trust others in ways I'd never trusted or depended on anyone else before. I mean an unconditional trust in others to help me overcome the physical limitations that resulted from my accident.

I learned a lot about myself and a lot about other people during my stay at West Florida. It sounds ironic when I say it out loud, but because of those relationships I formed and the experiences I endured during my stay, I decided that I guess hospitals aren't always as bad as people think they are.

———◇———

Caring Bridge Journal Entry by Amy Cozad — April 3, 2018

Welcome, friends and family! We will be using this Caring Bridge site to update you as Kyle continues to progress from inpatient to outpatient rehab, from small steps to big ones, and everything in between. We are truly beyond thankful for every single person who has called; sent a text, card, or email; or come by to visit. It is both encouraging and comforting to know he has such an incredible support team standing behind him.

With that being said, let's start with saying Kyle will get through this stronger and more resilient than he came into this season. We are grateful for the opportunity to strengthen, grow, and develop the skills necessary to master the physical therapy exercises he practices daily. In God's time, he will be back!

A quick backstory to get you up to speed: Kyle had a freak accident fall on Friday, March 16, in our home in Pensacola, Fla., causing a severe spinal cord injury. The GOOD NEWS is, even though this caused temporary loss of feeling in his legs and feet, the diagnosis was an "incomplete injury," meaning we could have a COMPLETE RECOVERY!! Kyle was taken to Sacred Heart Hospital the night of the incident and promptly had surgery the next day. He spent a few days recovering there and has since transferred to West Florida Rehabilitation Center, also here in Pensacola.

We have been adjusting well to the inpatient therapy at West Florida. Kyle is busy all seven days of the week, completing a strict regimen of physical and occupational therapy. He works hard to earn his new favorite cookies from Subway downstairs! We are projected to stay here until April 20 and will then be transferred to outpatient therapy and sent home! I will be working on my baking skills for the next few weeks to ensure my cookie recipes are up to Kyle's standards!! Currently, he has limited feeling in his legs, and we are still waiting for his feet to wake up. In one week, he has gone from not being able to stand to walking about thirty steps with the help of a standing table and his therapist! He is continuing to make small yet monumental improvements daily! Most importantly, his spirits remain high!

THANK YOU AGAIN for all the good wishes, prayers, and thoughtful notes! We are so blessed and thankful! However, our biggest and only request for now is to PLEASE KEEP THE PRAYERS COMING!! We are doing well managing meals, time, and the precious dogs! If anything changes or if we are in need of any assistance, I will be sure to update you all! May God bless each and every one of you. Thank you for your constant love and support as we transition through these next few months!

———◆———

CHAPTER 11

The Longest Month of My Life Begins

God's will is not automatic. He allows us to make choices.
Many of the things that happen to you are not God's perfect will.
We all have to choose between God's will and our will.

—Rick Warren

I must admit, one of the most positive and perhaps happiest moments during my recovery and my healing thought process occurred when I transferred from the hospital where I underwent my surgery and initial intensive care to my inpatient recovery hospital. I understand the amazing level of care I received and my incredible fortune for having the staff of surgeons and nurses caring for me immediately following my surgery. At the end of the day, that seemingly endless week in the hospital made me miserable, confined to bedrest, lying on my back with a revolving door of attentive nurses taking my vitals, attending to my pain, and trying to ensure I had the rest I needed following surgery. But I realized an incredible liberalization when I signed my discharge papers and was then given a short ambulance ride across town to the next step in my journey at West Florida Rehabilitation Center. There, the entire vibe of hospitalization, rehabilitation, and recovery took a turn in an incredibly positive direction.

I arrived Saturday and settled in. My occupational therapist—one of many that I'd soon consider a good friend—woke me.

He entered my room shortly after 7:00 a.m., looked around nonchalantly, and asked, "Where's your suitcase? You need to put on a pair of shorts and a T-shirt so we can get you up and out of bed."

Wow! After a week on my back, I wasn't sure I could even move, so the opportunity to get up, put on real clothes, and think about something other than lying still in bed was the best medicine I'd had to date.

For the next several weeks, especially as I look back on those initial days with my occupational and physical therapy teams, my progress seemed amazing. It far exceeded anything I initially imagined.

Amazing is a word that deserves context, especially in the new world I found myself in just one week after major surgery and now medically termed a paraplegic. I had little feeling below the waist. Although I had some movement of my lower legs, I had no feeling in my ankles and feet and a hollow numbness that made voluntary movement impossible at this stage of my treatment.

During my five weeks of inpatient rehabilitative therapy and even after going home, people kept reminding me to remember where I started and what I could or could not do on that first day there. In other words, don't think about what you used to be capable of doing. Instead, think about where you "restarted."

I found restarting an accurate description. In retrospect, after transferring to the West Florida Rehabilitation Center, it is extraordinarily humbling to think about all the things that I couldn't do for myself. I couldn't sit up by myself. I couldn't get in and out of the hospital bed without significant assistance. I couldn't even roll over in bed without help from one of my nurses. I couldn't dress and could barely feed myself. Life as I'd previously known it had to start over. That's a daunting task in front of someone with an uncertain future, but one thing helped to balance that fear of the unknown: the incredible patience, optimism, and professionalism of my therapy team at West Florida.

During my time as an inpatient rehabilitation patient, I accumulated many vivid memories, most of them what I called my "firsts." During my first few days there, they introduced me to a heavy mechanical jig that supported a patient's body weight and allowed the first step toward what I can only assume is every paraplegic's ultimate goal—to stand again. With the help of that large mechanical machine that was bolted to the floor, some heavy strapping that was secured around my waist, and a motor that could probably lift a pallet full of bricks, I looked in a mirror and watched myself in amazement as it pulled me out of my wheelchair and hoisted me to a standing position. That first attempt at standing up in my mechanical jig wasn't pretty to watch, but it really demonstrated a tangible first measure of progress that I truly appreciated.

Despite how crazy I probably looked during that initial attempt to stand, Amy might have had a tear or two in her eyes, so beauty really is in the eye of the beholder. Like with many of the exercises that I would do in the next month, I lacked balance and grace. But you know what? You have to start somewhere. After that initial physical therapy session, I stood. Between that mechanical contraption and my wobbling, it must have been ugly to watch, and I needed a lot of help in making it happen, but I was standing. I was on my way, baby!

———◇———

Weekly Wins!
Caring Bridge Journal Entry by Amy Cozad — April 6, 2018

Today marks the three-week point from Kyle's initial accident, but the daily progress we've seen during his initial days as an inpatient continues to lend room for optimism. Big ticket items for this week:

Kyle took his first assisted steps this week with his therapist and a large mobile machine called "ARJO." Amazing to think that just two weeks ago, he couldn't even stand, but now he's using his legs to stand and put together assisted steps to cross a small room.

He had all forty or so staples from his surgery removed on Wednesday. The wound has healed nicely, and with the additional mobility, the pain associated with the surgery seems to be diminishing.

With his staples gone, he's still required to wear his "torso shell" for stability and help in keeping his spinal column aligned for the next few months. Thankfully, he spends a large portion of his day sitting up in his wheelchair, which helps with strength and endurance. Wearing the brace is also becoming a bit more bearable (although he'll never admit that!) As his post-surgery pain begins to subside, he's sleeping well through the night—another significant change from his first week in the hospital!

A typical day at the rehab center includes several hours of occupational and physical therapy. We're blessed with a great team of docs, nurses, and therapists—that really helps with his positive outlook!

Based on his progress, his therapy team agrees that his discharge date from the West Florida Neurological Rehabilitation Center will be in two weeks (April 20). From major spinal surgery back to Quarters A in five weeks will be HUGE!

In preparation for his eventual transition home (where he'll move toward more outpatient PT), he was granted a field trip to the house with his occupational therapy team. From their perspective, the temporary quarters he'll initially occupy are suitable with some Americans with Disabilities Act compliance measures that will be implemented in the coming weeks. No showstoppers—AND the dogs enjoyed another chance to play with "Dad"!

Keep your prayers coming—it's humbling to realize how broad our Navy family really is and how unselfish that family is in offering anything from meals to dog sitting to prayers and well wishes! Thanks to each of you for your support.

————◇————

CHAPTER 12

Slow and Steady Wins the Race

*If you want to change your direction, if your time of life
is at hand, well, don't be the rule, be the exception.
A good way to start is to stand.*

—Winter Warlock, Santa Claus Is Coming to Town

It didn't take long for me to settle into the new inpatient rehab routine. I rose early in the morning every day for vital signs, a shower, and the daily visit by my doctor to discuss progress, concerns, and his overall assessment.

One thing I'll credit the entire staff at West Florida with is the fact that they always remained on the same page when it came to talking about a patient's future. The consistent theme for me regarding incomplete spinal injuries like mine meant they had no specific timeline that fit any one patient nor could anyone predict with any accuracy the extent of one's recovery. Everybody (and every body) heals in their own way and on their own timeline. More importantly, progress happens incrementally and often develops slowly.

One can find observing those small measures of progress frustrating, especially if you are the one who wants to see that progress happen now. So, I quickly realized I needed to learn the trait of patience. There were bound to be good days and better days, as Amy and I described them. With that mutual understanding, we refused to acknowledge anything less than a good day and agreed that every single day had something good that we could point to. In a world where we measure progress with such small improvements that aren't always apparent to the casual observer, recovery is as much about positive attitude and hard work as it is about physical effort. That positive attitude and hard work typically pays off in terms of a series of small gains that a patient accomplishes on his or her road to recovery.

Transferring from one sitting surface to another became another "first" for me. Little did I realize the first time I used a half-inch thick lacquered board to help facilitate movement from one place to another how foundational that skill was for someone in a wheelchair. The transfer board allowed me to slide from my bed to my wheelchair or to a physical therapy treatment bed. Eventually, I would use the transfer board to assist in getting in and out of our car. It soon became apparent that mastering the transfer board and moving from one surface to another provided a key first step in becoming independent. In a matter of days, my strength grew enough that I could transfer from my bed to my wheelchair without assistance. In a matter of weeks, I could get in and out of our car. It didn't take too much longer to eliminate the need for a transfer board at all. Whether I realized it at the time or not, those transfer steps gave me a big "first" that had me well on my way to independent wheelchair living.

During my inpatient stay, I also learned how to drive my new wheelchair—another one of those things that I'd never really thought about, and I'm here to tell you, it's not as simple as it looks, especially when you throw in thick carpet, uneven floor surfaces, and eventually steps and curbs. The therapy team is all about promoting a patient's independence, so Lord help me if they caught me allowing anyone to push me. When I first started to drive myself around, even though most of my therapy focused on my lower body, I would routinely go to bed at night with aching arms from pushing myself around the hospital. For the record, I still haven't come close to mastering anything that involves steps and curbs in the chair, but I have seen people do things in a wheelchair that make my mind spin.

One wheelchair skill required to do anything on uneven surfaces—whether that be a simple door transition that's only half an inch or a larger curb or step in a room—involves lifting the front wheels in a balanced motion. Think of doing a wheelie on your bike as a kid.

Every hour of physical therapy often felt like ten hours of hard work, both physically and often mentally demanding. Initially, I didn't find any of those physical therapy treatments fun, but learning to do wheelies broke that paradigm. It was just that—plain fun. Fun for me, that is, but Amy showed a bit more reluctance to acknowledge the fun, only thinking about a few close calls during my training. As an aviator, I was all in when asked if I was ready to try some of the balance drills required to lift my front wheels. Finally, something cool! And just like that little kid learning to ride a bike for the first time, I needed someone there to catch me when—not if—I fell. That's where I had complete trust in my therapist. Amy, on the other hand, might have sprouted a few gray hairs or skipped a few heartbeats watching me have my fun.

My medical team exercised great skill at having me focus on near-term goals as opposed to the obvious goal of walking independently again. Every day, the several hours spent on the therapy floor focused on building on every small improvement each patient had accomplished in previous days and weeks. The exercises concentrated on increased strength, improved flexibility, and better physical coordination. Even before my accident, I was never a limber person, so I didn't enjoy the flexibility exercises, but those paled in comparison to rebuilding all the physical coordination required to take steps again.

As a result of my injury, I had very little, if any, muscular control or feeling in my glutes. My hamstring and calf muscles were similarly lifeless. I had some sensation of pressure when the doctor touched these areas, but no feeling and certainly no muscular control. Surprisingly, though, I was fortunate to have complete feeling and fairly good muscular control in my quadricep muscles. So, building my therapy program became like directing a symphony of drummers with the string and brass sections in their seats but not able or caring to play along.

Thankfully, my therapy team amazed me as they built the elements required to take best advantage of the things that worked while compensating for the things that didn't. In addition to lacking feeling in much of my backside and legs, I had absolutely no feeling below my ankles in either of my feet. Think about walking without feeling your feet. Trust me—not only did I think about that often, but I had to figure out how to do it.

My daily physical therapy routine focused on re-teaching me how to compensate for my new lower body. Literally, I had to learn how to walk again—from scratch. That meant completely relearning the mechanics of walking, something that we all take for granted. Once I could stand in an upright position on that standing jig, my next step meant learning how to use a walker—but not the small, fragile aluminum walker that I had previously trained on. They showed me a much larger, more mechanical walker on wheels called an "ARJO." Given its physical size and stability, the ARJO reduces the risk of fall for the patient and allows a single therapist to get their patient to stand, balance, and eventually walk at what I considered a very early point in my therapy routine.

The ARJO had a belt and a motorized platform on which to rest one's upper body. The combination of the two served to assist you in standing from a seated position in a wheelchair, and then once you were standing, it provided the stability to help with balance and support when required. The first time they introduced me to what looks like an intimidating piece of gear, I almost pulled the walker over on top of me as I attempted to stand up with my six-foot-four-inch, 215-pound frame. It took three therapists to stabilize the machine and prevent it from tipping over with the full weight of my body as I tried to pull myself up. I relied on it completely to pull me up from my wheelchair and to hold me up on the legs I couldn't feel (and certainly couldn't control). But once I was up, it was another of those amazing, indescribable feelings. Standing again. Well, kind of. Another small step on the road to recovery.

But standing was only part of the battle. Next, I had to completely relearn the mechanics of walking—one of those things we instinctively do without considering how. The mechanics of extending your knee while shifting your weight to the opposite hip and advancing one foot ahead of the other. Simple, right? One would think so, but I can tell you that I've never had to concentrate so hard on something so seemingly simple in my life. I had to talk each leg through each one of the mechanical procedures to put one foot in front of the other. I had to watch my foot placement, since I had very little control and had no perception of how big one step was compared to the next. I had to keep an eye on my feet, since I had this crazy tendency for my toes to point perpendicular to my direction of travel.

Relearning how to walk became the most difficult thing I've ever done, but I kept remembering the words from a song in a Christmas special we used to watch every year when I was a kid. In one scene, the main character, Kris Kringle, attempts to teach the mythical Winter Warlock how to walk. To aid in his teaching, the main character starts singing, "You put one foot in front of the other, and soon you'll be walking across the floor." Ah, if it were only that easy.

I find it funny how our competitive nature seems to kick in at the most unusual times in our lives. As I became stronger, every day, I would start off my therapy session on the walker. As I started out, I would have to concentrate so hard on hip place-ment, knee alignment, weight distribution, and step mechanics that I wouldn't talk while I walked. Maybe some irony with the old saying, "You can't walk and chew gum at the same time"? At any rate, Amy would count my steps—the physical num-ber of foot movements I'd made. My therapist would count the number of linear feet I had walked based on the number of tiles on the floor. At the end, Amy would correct my therapist on distance. I'd just smile, a bit tired from the walk but know-ing full well they were each measuring something different. But as I smiled, I did so knowing that I had just done better than I'd done the day before. That's all that I worried about—make today better than yesterday.

I learned how to lift my feet, at first in inches and eventually enough that I didn't have to pick them up with my hands to put them into my wheelchair foot rests. Day by day, I became stronger in my mechanical steps. Soon, I transitioned from that ARJO machine to a lightweight walker.

At first, it only took five or six steps before exhaustion set in. Ironically, since I had difficulty with my standing balance, my upper body became exhausted, not my legs. These steps took a lot of brain power as well because I had to think through each step. My mind and body timing had to relearn, so I experienced mental exhaustion as well. But with some hard work and persistence, I increased my endurance to over 100 steps. My strength increased daily, and although my lack of feeling below my waist didn't improve much, with the help of my occupational and physical therapy team, I grew in my ability to compensate for that lack of feeling, coordination, and muscular strength. That slow but measurable progress felt great.

All in all, I relearned enough and became strong enough to earn my release in just over four weeks. At that point, my doctors and therapy team expressed confidence that, with assistance, I could safely live at home in a controlled environment (with some supervision). For that release, they emphasized safety in basic movements and daily routine rather than taking steps or standing up. Those would hopefully continue to improve with time. I still needed help dressing and doing many of my day-to-day routines, but looking back at my first day, I had shown an incredible amount of progress. Yes, progress that amounted to relearning many basic life skills, but I was not even close to being able to feel and walk again. Nonetheless, I found this major step encouraging, especially for a guy whom doctors didn't ever expect to get out of a wheelchair. I looked so forward to going home again—well, at least almost home.

———◇———

Learning to Be Patient
Caring Bridge Journal Entry by Amy Cozad – April 15, 2018

One of the hardest traits to learn, especially for a Type A naval aviator, is "patience." Fortunately, our team of incredible occupational and physical therapists has helped to focus our vision on the many small steps required to achieve the progress that Kyle is so laser focused on.

Focus continues on strengthening and fine-tuning muscle coordination. Although in Kyle's words, "I may not be earning too many style points," his step coordination shows improvement each and every day.

In addition to greater endurance on the bulky, mechanical "ARJO" walking machine, Kyle stood up (no small feat, given his height) and took his first steps in a more traditional aluminum walker earlier this week. In just a matter of days, he walked over twenty steps in the walker. He keeps telling us there is "no quit in a Cozad"—this is proof positive.

He's also using an electronic bike that actually stimulates his muscles during every cycling motion. When a muscle should be firing, an electrical impulse is generated to assist in recovery. I have almost earned my "operators qual" to hook him up and get him peddling. So far, so good!

He'll be released as a "graduate" of the inpatient program and will transition to outpatient spinal rehab patient status next Friday, so work on a small office/bedroom is underway to be ready for his arrival. Until he can climb the over thirty steps to get up to our bedroom, he'll have a nice man cave adjacent to our garage that will have everything he needs—including dog beds for Charlie and Cooper!

Keep the prayers and positive thoughts coming...they are making a difference!

—————◆—————

CHAPTER 13

Home At Last (Almost)

I'm on my way, I'm on my way home sweet home.

—Mötley Crüe

Life as a flag officer in the United States Navy sometimes has a perk or two associated with it. "Rank has its privileges," as the saying goes. Admittedly, any perks go hand in hand with the hard work and long hours required of seniority that takes years in the making.

In Pensacola, I served as the highest-ranking active-duty officer on the Naval Air Station—and in the entire region for that matter. As a result of my seniority, the base afforded my wife and I incredible quarters during our assignment. Quite honestly, calling our residence a mere house seems an understatement. They placed us in an incredible, historic masterpiece dating back to its original construction in the early 1800s when Pensacola functioned as a naval shipyard.

The house, known as "Quarters A," had once been occupied by Confederate troops during the Civil War. They'd burned it to the ground as those same troops retreated from what we know today as Naval Air Station Pensacola. Fortunately, the navy yard rebuilt the home to its present grand state, and it's maintained in pristine condition today as an artifact of the National Registry of Historic Homes. It has provided a temporary military residence to some amazing names in naval history, such as Nimitz, Read, and Halsey. Quarters A also served as the centerpiece for Pensacola's transition from a ship building yard to one of our Navy's initial naval air stations back in 1910. Today, Pensacola continues to be the "Cradle of Naval Aviation," since every prospective naval aviator, future pilot, naval flight officer, and enlisted aviation specialist starts their humble beginnings in Pensacola.

Before my accident, I looked at the magnificence of the house in completely different terms. I looked at it from the perspective of its history, its incredible architecture, and its mammoth square footage (that also included summer air conditioning bills). That was my "before" perspective—one that changed dramatically when I returned home from the hospital. Now in a wheelchair, that perspective instantly shifted as I took in the reality of my new nemesis—stairs.

You see, just to get to the first level, our entertaining level, I would have to climb ten stairs. Then, to sleep in my own bed, I would have to ascend another twenty-three stairs to reach the living floor with our main bedrooms. As you can imagine, stairs and wheelchairs don't go together so well (at least for a new user). So, until I figured out how to get up and down the stairs, I took up living in our guest quarters as a temporary measure. This fifteen-foot-by-twenty-foot combination of office, bedroom, and bathroom would remain my new home, at least until I could figure out how to conquer those steps required to get back to really living in the historic home I loved.

During this portion of my ongoing recovery, I slept, showered, ate, and worked in my new one-room home. A story in and of itself, this single room adjacent to the main house had been previously used as an enlisted aide office. Now, with the addition of a wheelchair ramp and some Americans with Disabilities Act compliant hardware in the small bathroom, it was perfect for my needs. I could change clothes, shower, and work in my hospital bed with an iPad or from my desktop sitting in my wheelchair. I also had a TV in the room, so when I look back on my total time spent in the ICU, in patient rehab, and during those first days back in the house, I can admit that I watched every single major sporting event known to man (and some others that I'm quite certain are not known to anyone other than me).

After returning home, I still went back to West Florida, where I attended outpatient physical therapy three times each week and continued exercises in my small room to keep improving my strength and mobility. But I also focused on two other important aspects of my recovery: getting back to work in my role as commander of the Naval Education and Training Command, and on a more personal basis, re-establishing a new normal for Amy and me.

————◇————

There's No Place Like Home
Caring Bridge Journal Entry by Amy Cozad — April 22, 2018

So, after just over four weeks to the day, Kyle is able to return home to continue the great rehab work in an outpatient status over the coming months. The good news is that we have him home where he belongs. The bad news is, since we live in a historic home that requires ten steep steps just to get up to the kitchen and entertaining floor, he's got his own "man cave" in an in-law suite that's just outside the main house.

I was able to get a second bed, so I will be spending lots of time out there with him. Our base housing team did a great short-term rehab on the room to get wheelchair ramps, shower accessories, and a work computer all set up. He's got direct access to the backyard and back patio—so much nicer than his previous "digs."

After getting home late yesterday afternoon, he's already cooked steaks on the grill and wheeled himself along with the dogs and me on a walk down by the sea wall, and we're off for a "real haircut" later this afternoon.

Hard work continues to prevail in rehab. I am qualified to set up an electronic stimulation bike that he'll ride every day we visit West Florida Rehabilitation Center. The bike is pretty amazing as it stimulates the "right muscle—at the right time" to peddle the bike, hopefully helping to awaken those leg areas that are still not fully responsive.

He's also over doubled his walker distance in five days this last week (now about fifty feet). At home, we'll continue to work on exercises that push endurance and that complement what the therapists will challenge him to do in coming weeks. Rest this weekend is good, but we're really just rebuilding what a "normal" day looks like (to include his work at the Naval Education and Training Command in small, progressive chunks).

Keep the prayers and positive vibes coming as we make this next transition...we've likely entered the slow and patient portion of his therapy, but he grits his teeth every morning, committed to doing more than he did the day before.

———◆———

Getting Used to Our "New Normal"
Caring Bridge Journal Entry by Amy Cozad — April 30, 2018

So, just over a week ago, we were released from West Florida Rehab Hospital and allowed to return home. I guess for clarification—halfway home since Kyle's staying in our staff office turned guest quarters off the main house until he can climb the multiple stairs that get him "all the way home."

Regardless, it's good to be here. And it's good for me (Amy) since I just need to walk out and see Kyle as opposed to driving back and forth every day. We spent a fair amount of time last week with follow-up appointments, doctors' referrals, and finalizing medical equipment approval, so not as "relaxing" as one would think. Hopefully, that normalizes itself a bit in the coming weeks.

Kyle also got an electronic bone stimulator that attaches to the front of his protective shell. He wears this two hours each day, as the stimulation enhances the body's natural tendency to bond bone to surgical "hardware"—we're hopeful this is 100 percent successful!

Monday is our first follow-up appointment with Kyle's surgeon since his surgery on March 17th. We're optimistic that he's healing well and that we'll get good news tomorrow.

Monday also marks his return to physical therapy—this time, as an outpatient. Three hours per week with a therapist, and three more hours available on the electrical stimulation bike at our discretion. With all the other admin "distractions" this past week, he's anxious to get started.

This past week marked the Maritime Patrol Association's annual reunion in Jacksonville. Although we couldn't be there, someone made a sign that said, "RADM Cozad and Awesome Amy—Wish You Were Here!" We must have received two dozen pictures through the week of people sending copies of them posing with the sign...it's the prayers and thoughtful actions like this that really help the attitude stay positive!

We're assuming that things will slow down a bit as we get to that point where the progress will be a bit less dramatic than it was in rehab. Keep those prayers coming. We're blessed to have such an incredible network of friends and family sharing in this journey!

———◇———

HSM-72 Deployment Homecoming, Naval Air Station
Jacksonville, FL—walking the flight line to greet my son,
just as Amy had promised I'd do while still in the hospital.

Anniversary date night out on the town in Pensacola just five months after the accident and surgery.

"Where there is a will, there is a way." Newport, RI—visiting the Navy's Command Leadership School. Due to rain, there were no handicapped accessible ramps that weren't flooded!

Relearning how to climb stairs during one of many hundreds of hours of arduous physical and occupational therapy.

Recruit Training Command Graduation, Great Lakes, IL—my first airline travel and first public speaking opportunity after the accident.

Navy Wounded Warrior team tryouts in San Diego, CA. Ironically, I had never really played tennis before…until then.

With Jon Stewart at the 2019 Department of Defense Warrior Games in Tampa, FL.

July 9, 2020—retirement ceremony with Amy. It was pretty special to retire at the National Naval Aviation Museum (with only ten guests allowed due to COVID), knowing at that time that I would soon become the President and CEO of the Naval Aviation Museum Foundation in Pensacola.

In the ICU with my grandson Jaxon just days after my accident and surgery. I had no idea what the future held…

West Florida Hospital—this was the first time I was able to see our dogs, Charlie and Cooper, since being hospitalized. They weren't quite sure what to think about my new "ride."

Jaxon with his "Pop Pop" buddy doll. It's amazing how much little ones like him really comprehend life's challenges.

Remote working from the home office (aka "the man cave") during COVID as I continued with my recovery and return to full-time duty.

Amy speaking at the 2019 Pensacola area Military Spouse Appreciation Luncheon. Needless to say, she has become a unique example of strength, grace, and love for those in our community and in our Navy.

My first time cooking after coming home and mastering the ten stairs to get into historic Quarters A. Note my four-legged helpers. Here, my "new normal" felt anything BUT normal.

Sacred Heart Hospital ICU— despite the pain and post-op disorientation, I was still able to muster a smile.

Back at work! I surprised many with how quickly I was able to return to work and travel to see one of the hundreds of schoolhouses and great leaders who fell under my command at the Naval Education and Training Command.

Pretty sure I can say with confidence that I'm the only guy in a wheelchair to get to blow up explosives at the Navy's Explosive Ordnance Disposal School. Oohrah, heroes!

I got to the point that I could shift my weight to steer my wheelchair down almost any ramp. That still mortifies Amy as I go down the airport jet bridge to board our airplanes—especially with the flight attendants watching!

Grand Marshal for the Annual Fiesta Pensacola Parade. Jaxon had emptied his bag of beads thrown to parade watchers within the first 100 yards!

The oldest (and most senior) gold medalist at the 2019 Department of Defense Warrior Games.

The new normal. Not sure who was more excited about learning how to drive again—me or the pups. I know I wasn't too excited when I was told I had to take another driver's test (at the age of 57!)

I can't tell you how humbling (and inspiring) it was for everyone on Team Navy to have support from two of our Navy's finest enlisted leaders at the Department of Defense Warrior Games in Tampa!

Back at work—or, as Amy called it during my initial days in the office, "daddy daycare" because she could leave me in the able hands of my staff and catch a break after months of attending to me.

Navy Ball in Newport, RI. At this point of my journey, I was able to talk about my accident and recovery as I traveled on work-related business. I still don't consider myself inspirational or unique compared to others who have suffered similar life-altering injuries. Sometimes, you just have to be tougher than your circumstances.

Warrior Ride in Pensacola. Amy's been by my side (or in the seat behind me) every second of every day. I'm one lucky man!

Opening Ceremonies of the Department of Defense Warrior Games. This photo speaks volumes to Amy's role as a leader, a friend, and a medical caregiver. Here, she helps lead Team Navy into Amalie Arena. Note the "boot" on my right foot. To this day, I'm not sure how I broke it, but I participated in the Warrior Games with a broken foot!

Speaking at a public event held at the
National Naval Aviation Museum
(January 2022).

CHAPTER 14

The Hardest Job

Step into my shoes and walk the life I'm living. If you get
as far as I have, you'll know how strong I really am.

—Anonymous Caregiver

I've run across a lot of friends and professional acquaintances who remind me how impressive my progress appears to be and how well I'm doing under tough personal circumstances. Many will also anchor on how they've received inspiration from the way I've approached my recovery. I think about that every now and then, and although it's nice to know that people appreciate the challenges and difficulty of this journey, I've found this hard to accept. I typically respond the same way to each one of those well-wishers: In all honesty, I know how hard I've worked toward my continued recovery, but comparatively, I have the easy job. I am working hard to balance the new normal of home exercise, physical therapy, getting back into work in my Navy job, and most importantly, maintaining my relationship with my family. But those facets of my new life are natural and seem easy. Amy is the one who has really stepped up to tackle what I consider the hardest job.

I found that the need for a personal support network during my hospitalization helped carry me through what I considered the most difficult period of my recovery. For most, this support typically comes from family or close friends who are there to encourage anyone who's suffered a significant injury beyond what the medical staff can provide. When I awoke from surgery, I realized my luck in having Amy with me that day and every day of my hospitalization, including the majority of my occupational and physical therapy sessions. In addition to all those roles I've mentioned, she's also fulfilled the role as my spiritual mentor. It was nothing short of inspirational to have her by my side given the strength that she had displayed during this challenging time.

Amy could always find something good in any situation, regardless of how small or seemingly insignificant. She would push me more than I thought I could push myself. And she always provided an incredible optimism to our long-term recovery prognosis. In Amy's words, "We will make a full recovery. We just don't know what that really means." Without a doubt, she has been the single most important influence on my ability to stay positive during a time that many would assume was dark and filled with emotionally challenging feelings.

Unfortunately, for a variety of reasons, not everyone has local family that are available or willing to participate as actively as Amy participated in my hospitalization and rehabilitation. Some patients don't have options for a local rehabilitation hospital and are required to travel hours away from home for their inpatient recovery. Others might not have the support of friends or family able or willing to take time off to come help. At the end of the day, not everyone has the same close family ties with which I am blessed. I witnessed, firsthand, the difference in patient attitude, optimism, and progress with those fortunate enough to have a strong support network and, sadly, those who were forced to go at it alone.

The West Florida Rehabilitation Center was no exception. Not everyone had an "Amy" there to support their recovery, and I'm sure it's that way in other rehabilitation centers. I saw the difference in those whose family or close friends attended their treatment sessions every day. I could see a difference in those who had someone to talk to in their hospital room during the sparse hours they weren't scheduled for a treatment. It's hard enough to imagine the difficulty in facing a catastrophic injury or life-threatening medical diagnosis. Just think about the difficulty in tackling that on your own.

For me, the support I received from coworkers, friends, and family served to motivate me and helped me maintain a consistently positive attitude, regardless of how the day had gone. On those good days, maybe I didn't need as many pep talks or as much of the encouragement that really helped me along on the rare bad days. More than a few times, I woke up in the morning not too excited about the schedule that the day ahead held for me, but knowing that I'd have Amy there to help me tackle the challenges head on made it bearable. That support was—and continues to be—the foundation for the tough façade that I try hard to demonstrate every day, no matter what challenges lay ahead of me.

That need for support doesn't stop upon a patient's discharge from the hospital. I know I certainly didn't anticipate how hard it would actually be to leave the hospital and go home. Don't get me wrong—I wanted to get out of there, but until I went home, I didn't understand how important a role my nurses and medical technicians played in helping me achieve my daily routine while at West Florida.

In many ways, going home seemed comparable to getting paroled from prison for good conduct, although I should emphasize that I've never been to prison, so I guess I don't know firsthand what being paroled feels like. Having said that, it seems like you look forward to the day, but when it actually arrives, it's a bit terrifying. This forced me to face the fact that I'd have to figure out how to get things done after having lost the ability to do many things for myself.

In addition to modifying our house to include things like wheelchair ramps, handicapped rails, and other equipment, I needed someone to help with the things I couldn't yet do for myself. Simple things like dressing, showering, and using the restroom proved infinitely more difficult. All the while, I was still required to wear my protective turtle shell, which complicated everything to the next level. Although my hospital team expressed comfort in my readiness for the next step in my recovery, I could count multiple tasks that were just plain impossible for me to do for myself.

As we left the hospital for the last time in my former inpatient status, Amy and I faced the challenge of realigning our entire day, each and every day of the week, around my new physical limitations. Before my injury, Amy had settled into the Pensacola military community and wanted to jump back into the local school system, where she taught special education at the elementary grade level. She also enjoyed traveling to see her folks, our two daughters, and our grandson at every opportunity during my busy work weeks. My injury, and more so the care I required to get through each day, changed all that. Amy willingly recognized her new full-time role as my primary medical caregiver.

It's hard to even wrap my mind around the commitment and unselfish love she's demonstrated every single day while assuming the role of primary medical caregiver, a title added to the list of wife, mother, grandma, and Navy spouse. I try to say thank you every single day, and while I could never find a physical gift to repay her for the sacrifices, she will acknowledge what I can do: Continue to work hard at my therapy. Make my recovery my number one priority above work. And continue to take one step further today than I did yesterday. It may not sound like much, but that's what she deserves.

I get a chuckle when I tell people that, although it's far from the truth, I used to tease Amy that she was high mainte-nance. Well, you've all heard the adage that "he who laughs last, laughs loudest." In our house, we have maintained the ability to demonstrate a rich sense of humor, so clearly today, Amy has had the last laugh. Without question, Kyle Cozad has become the high maintenance award winner in our family. As a result, Amy (and every other family member who has assumed the heroic role of being a primary medical caregiver) has earned my eternal thanks. Without any doubt, I couldn't get along without the caregiver support Amy provides every day.

At our home, since I'm unable to assist in many of the daily chores, Amy still minds the house, does laundry, cooks, and cleans. She carries the burden of my chores as well, although she'd tell you that I never really did anything before I got hurt. I take that in jest, but she really sounds serious when she tells people this.

Although I've become much more independent since first coming home, I can't do it without her. Quite honestly, nobody really thinks about the caregiver or what they've given up by providing the support they do for a loved one. But I can tell you firsthand, on this journey of recovery in the Cozad house, Amy has by far the most difficult job.

———◇———

Settling Back In at Home
Caring Bridge Journal Entry by Amy Cozad — May 6, 2018

Looking back, it's amazing how busy our "new normal" life is... maybe not busy in the sense of numbers of appointments or outings but in terms of the time it takes us to get ready! That said, we're getting to be a good team at getting ready, getting in/out of the car, finding time for extra exercises at home, and don't forget meals. It has been great being able to spend time together. [Note from Kyle: Amy's too modest to talk about how busy SHE is...still keeping the house pristine, running the inevitable unexpected trip to the store, taking dogs to the groomer, etc. She's an amazing lady, and none of my small victories would be possible without her!]

The week started with x-rays and Kyle's first post-surgery follow-up with his neurosurgeon. His doctor was very happy with progress to date—the incision area has healed nicely, and x-rays revealed that the bone/titanium fusion is progressing very well. He's got good alignment, and as painful as his "torso shell" and two hours of daily bone stimulation vest are, it is paying positive dividends. Next appointment—June 22. Hopefully, that'll be the last he'll see of his torso vest. That alone will be a tremendous change to our daily routine, since EVERY time he gets out of bed—whether that's to sit at the desk, go outside with the dogs, eat lunch, or take a shower—it requires me to help him buckle into his shell. Cross your fingers and say your prayers!

We are back in the full swing of physical therapy three times per week. Kyle has one very intense hour with his therapist each visit, followed by an hour on the electrical stimulation bike. He continues to gain more stamina on the walker (ninety small steps with his walker in one effort this week), but his therapy is also focused on retraining muscles and reflexes that were impacted by his accident. His physical therapy motto: Make every day better than the last!

And as if things aren't busy enough, we've both been planning for next week's "big event." Next week marks the annual Aviation Flag Officer and Retired Flag Officer Training Symposium here in Pensacola, so we're gearing up to host around 200 active duty and retired aviation flag officers and spouses for a welcome social at our house. Full disclosure: We're catering the event and have tons of help, but with everything else going on, we'll both be glad to see many good friends again and will breathe a sigh of relief when it's all over. [Note from Kyle: It should be no surprise that Amy is doing all the work—again!]

But...with all the new business in our lives, Kyle got "dressed up" and took me to dinner for the first time out and about at a nice restaurant since his accident. It was great to get out and really continue to build on our new "normal." We had so much fun that I know this will become part of our normal routine—just like our weekend walks with the dogs down near the base seawall.

We continue to feel blessed with the daily improvements that we're seeing in strength, flexibility, and mobility. Mind you—he's got a long way to go...Kyle likes to compare his road ahead as taking a rowboat from San Diego to Tokyo and measuring progress in terms of inches as opposed to miles. He's optimistic—he won't let anything dampen his spirits, and although we realize there is a long recuperative road ahead, he and I continue to be "all in" for his recovery, however that may be defined. Kyle's grown very fond of a poster that states: "There is no ONE giant step that does it...it takes a lot of little steps," so as always, please keep those prayers coming!

—◆—

CHAPTER 15

The New Normal

*What lies behind you and what lies in front of you pales
in comparison to what lies inside of you.*

—Ralph Waldo Emerson

It's probably not hard for anyone to imagine that, soon after
my accident, life as Amy and I had known it became completely different from what we knew during our initial thirty-three years of marriage—at least for the time being. Weeks
before our discharge from West Florida, our therapy team had
done a great job beginning to set our expectations for the big
return home. One of the areas that neither of us really considered before we began discussing with our therapy team was
how to make life seem normal again. Although it didn't seem
intuitive, limiting visits by any well-wishers, friends, and even
family until we had settled into a routine became one of their
best recommendations.

So, all that sounded nice and easy. Like riding a bike, it
should be almost second nature. Step one: Get back home to
those familiar surroundings and look to live life as we had before.

Of course, given my medical condition and inability to access the main house, we simply didn't have the option of living as we had before. So, step one really boiled down to establishing what normal looked like post-accident.

Step two had equal complications after defining normal under our new limitations and actually establishing a new routine. It wouldn't be the normal we used to know but something new and very, very different.

Simple things like getting the day started seemed to take hours. Since Amy slept in the main house most nights of the week, she assumed my previous duties of getting up, taking the dogs outside first thing in the morning, and then feeding them. Then came the real work—getting me out of bed, shaved, showered, and dressed for the day. It's ironic how something that sounds so simple could take hours to accomplish under the circumstances in which we found ourselves.

By the time I had cleaned up and gotten ready for the day, Amy would head back into the main house to start her daily routine. By then, lunch time would have arrived, and then we'd leave for physical therapy three times each week. By the time we'd finished the therapy appointment and returned home, it would be time for Amy to prepare dinner and deliver it to my home away from home outside the main quarters. Throw in the inevitable and always inconvenient visit to the hospital urgent care medical site, and we didn't think this new life would ever feel anything less than exhausting. Geez, who ever imagined that our new normal would involve so many complicating and time-consuming procedures? We weren't sure during those first few weeks that we'd ever get anything done outside of getting dressed, eating, attending physical therapy, and starting over for the next day.

We spent many hours every day in that temporary one-room living quarters that I called home for the first few months. I was there because I didn't have a choice, and Amy was there simply so we could spend time together. Far from fancy by any means, the walls were a stark white with the only color in the room coming from a blue fabric armchair that we'd imported from the main house so Amy could sit and watch TV with me. I looked forward to her frequent visits, and more so to the weekends when she would sleep next to me on a rented rollaway bed. She was such a trooper, as I knew how uncomfortable that bed must have felt by the way she moaned in the morning when she got out of it. But in time, even our dogs became accustomed to having a bed in my room and spent hours upon hours with me to keep me company while Amy did other chores around the house or tried to capture five minutes when she could just put up her feet, close her eyes, and relax.

We embraced that change, and after a few short weeks, we figured out our new routine. I said shortly after the accident that I realized how lucky I was, and it might sound ironic, but we both felt fortunate to be back in our home (kind of) and to be able to spend time together each day. We remained thankful for the daily progress and for our ability to do things that we hadn't been able to do while I was in the hospital. That being said, after settling into our new routine, we started to expand our comfort zone. It didn't take long before we resumed our regular date nights and tested our ability to get back into town, get the car parked, get me loaded into the wheelchair, and get me into a restaurant. We refused to let anyone tell us, "You can't do that."

As if our new life wasn't complicated enough, just two short weeks after my release from inpatient rehabilitation, we did the unimaginable. We actually opened our home to over 200 aviation flag officers (admirals) and spouses, including the Chief of Naval Operations and the newly confirmed Undersecretary of the Navy during the annual Aviation Flag Officer Training Symposium in Pensacola. Trust me, we had plenty of friends try to convince us that we didn't need to host this event under the circumstances. For those of you asking, "How did you cook for all those folks?" Actually, one aspect of our new normal included a very liberal use of catering. But in all seriousness, that evening—as crazy as many thought it sounded when we said, "Yeah, we're going to do this"—became another important step in our return back to normal. In retrospect, it held some incredibly essential therapeutic value for each of us. It demonstrated to Amy and me that, despite the injury, our life seemed almost as normal that day as several weeks prior to my accident. That sense of normalcy came at a time when we both really needed it. Recollecting on the event that next day, still tired from a long night of talking to old friends, really reinforced for both of us that we could do this.

Equally important, that night offered a great opportunity for me to see old friends and for them to see each of us for the first time since my accident, news of which had spread quickly within the flag officer wardroom, as we call it. I found the outpouring of prayers, well wishes, and offers of support both humbling and overwhelming. The largest component of support came from my aviation brothers and sisters, so hosting that huge event at Quarters A, regardless of how crazy it sounded at the time, gave us our first chance to say thanks to each of them. It also gave me a chance to break the ice and get out in a social setting.

To be honest, venturing out and mingling with friends felt awkward and uncomfortable for me once I found myself confined to a wheelchair. At that time during my recovery, sitting in my wheelchair for more than two hours tended to cause a fair bit of lower back pain, but I toughed it out that night for nearly double that time because I was having so much fun. That night became an important first step in helping me regain my confidence to mingle and to make appearances in public as the most recognizable flag officer in the Navy confined to a wheelchair. Of course, I was also the only Navy admiral confined to a wheelchair.

——◆——

Mother's Day "Off"
Caring Bridge Journal Entry by Kyle Cozad — May 14, 2018

Since yesterday was Mother's Day, I wanted to give Amy a break, so Kyle will be writing this week's update. As you would imagine, if there were a theme to my message, it would focus on the incredible woman I married more than thirty-two years ago. The same lady who raised three incredible kids who are each successful in their own adult lives, and the same lady who is "Mimi" to an amazing little grandson in Memphis.

With that in mind, it should come as no surprise that "we" (code for Amy) hosted an incredible open house last Tuesday. Having a few folks over for cocktails is one thing, but having over 200 aviation flag officers and spouses over is serious business. In that group were our Under Secretary of the Navy, the Chief of Naval Operations, and the Commander of U.S. Pacific Command. The night was as good as I've ever seen due to Amy's planning and love for details—all the while caring for me along the way. Reconnecting with awesome friends was great "therapy" for us and helped to continue to set our new normal. What an amazing lady.

It's important to highlight that just four hours prior to the masses descending on Quarters A, Amy insisted (like only she can do) on taking me to one of my three physical therapy sessions for the week. What an incredible lady.

As has become par for the course, she didn't blink at the unplanned doctors' appointments or the Saturday visit to urgent care (nothing serious, but I'm telling you—I have spent more time with doctors in the past sixty days than I have in my entire thirty-three-year Navy career). Amy never hesitates—she helps me get dressed (code for ensuring my shorts and shirt match), helps me in/out of the car, and waits in long lines for the inevitable prescription. What an incredible lady.

Mother's Day was quiet but an opportunity to shower her with cards and gifts that will never adequately tell her how much I appreciate what she does during these uncertain times. She's my best nurse, at-home therapist, and cheerleader. I can't tell you how many steps I pounded out using my walker today (but she can), but I'll admit something. Today, we worked with a different therapist than we usually work with. When she asked, "How do you determine how far you aim to go each day—is it to improve your personal best?" I said yes, but really—I take each one of those steps for Amy...

She's an incredible lady. Happy Mother's Day! Thanks for

the continuing prayers!!! It's amazing to have friends supporting us like you all have.

———◆———

CHAPTER 16

Every Superman Needs a Wonder Woman

*My most brilliant achievement was my ability
to be able to persuade my wife to marry me.*

—Winston Churchill

I've become good friends with many of the staff at West Florida Rehabilitation Center as a result of the extensive time that I spent there following my accident. One of those good friends is an impressive young lady who works at the valet parking desk. If there is one person who really has a chance to present a positive first impression to visitors, regardless of whether it's their first or one hundredth visit, she is the one. She channels an energy and positivity that every patient or family member coming to visit a loved one really benefits from in a hospital setting like this. Everyone appreciates her friendly face, her kind greetings, and most importantly, her infectiously upbeat attitude. Rain or shine, whether you're in a good mood or you have the proverbial weight of the world on your shoulders, the positive vibe she projects really makes a noticeable difference for everyone.

We first became acquaintances when I lived in the inpatient ward, undergoing daily occupational and physical therapy sessions. When we'd finished for the day, I'd often ask Amy to bring me outside so I could enjoy the sunshine and get some fresh air that I missed while confined to my hospital room for much of the day. I'm not sure why I craved that, but I have a suspicion that the protective polyurethane shell the doctor required me to wear every time I was out of bed had something to do with it. If you remember, the shell served the purpose of keeping my upper body rigid and ensuring my spinal alignment remained intact during the critical initial phases of the healing process. That said, one can imagine the discomfort I experienced having that contraption locked onto my body and the heat it trapped in during the rising temperatures of the Florida panhandle.

Every time we'd go outside, the young lady at the valet parking desk would be sitting there with a smile and kind greeting. It didn't take long before that kind greeting became a standard question: "How's my Superman, today?"

Admittedly, for a guy who couldn't initially sit up in bed on his own, take three consecutive steps in a mechanical walker, or even lift his own legs onto the hospital bed, being called "Superman" certainly built my confidence. Having someone call me "Superman" when I was feeling drained after a tough therapy session gave me the ego boost I needed. To this day, when I arrive for a workout, aqua therapy, or one of my scheduled physical therapy appointments, I'm still greeted with that same smile and the welcome that will never get old: "There goes my Superman!"

I'm no comic book fan, but if I were, I'm sure I'd come

to realize that for every Superman, there is a Wonder Woman. From the moment she saw me on the floor that night in our home and called 911 emergency medical services, Mrs. Amy Louise Cozad has been, without question, my rock, my foundation, and yes, my Wonder Woman. People often ask how I stay so positive and so strong with the uncertainty of ever walking normally again. I don't even need to think about that one. Amy has provided the forcing function from the moment I was rolled into the operating room. She always puts my recovery in terms of "when," not "if." She's stood by me for nearly every one of my therapy sessions along the way and sets typically ridiculous goals that always seem unattainable. Of course, with my driven personality, I always try to beat those seemingly impossible goals.

Many folks will ask me about the so-called bad days along the way. Every time I get that question, I honestly can't recall any truly bad days along the way. Yes, we've both had some heavy thoughts. We've experienced frustration with certain elements of my recovery. Any injury and recovery that changes collective lives will certainly present an emotional roller coaster for those involved. But at the end of the day, Amy and I have really leaned on each other to stay strong. My kids fondly refer to this as #CozadStrong. Maybe that's not overly original, but it fits. The key to #CozadStrong is Amy's strength and optimism. She won't allow me to get down. She always finds the good in every single situation we find ourselves in. Without a doubt, she's my Wonder Woman.

As I talk about my own experiences with others who are facing similar injuries and challenging rehabilitation, I tell them that I've had a few key elements that really enable the relentless positivity that someone once used to describe me. Without a doubt, the number one enabler has been my ability to remain close to family. Amy went with me to the hospital. She waited for me in the emergency room waiting area. She's attended nearly every single occupational and physical therapy session that I've endured. She's served as my cheerleader and my coach, and at times, she has delivered a much deserved, "Stop feeling sorry for yourself." It's hard for me to imagine going through what I've gone through without someone as strong as Amy, who has constantly stood by my side. I only hope that any glimmers of strength that I've shown her along this journey have had half the impact that my Wonder Woman has had on me.

---◆---

It Takes a Team
Caring Bridge Journal Entry by Amy Cozad – May 26, 2018

So, the past two weeks have really felt like we have settled into our new normal. Multiple "date nights" where we're getting out of the house and trying new local restaurants, grocery shopping (Kyle has become my "cart" to carry everything), and even dress shopping for a speaking engagement that I had this past week. I'm happy to report that—with the exception of a short follow-up visit—we've NOT had any annoying visits to urgent care on the weekends or regularly scheduled doctors' visits, so we're hoping his body is finally "settling in" and all systems are functioning normally—well, he says, "most systems!" We've really come to learn that, as much as Kyle depends on me for support these days, I depend on him… "Team Cozad" is a term that we've often used during our thirty-three years of military service (22 May was his USNA graduation anniversary!), but it has a more profound meaning now...

Physical therapy continues to progress with new skills learned with every session. Over the last few weeks, he has increased his walker endurance to 200 steps—almost fifty greater than his previous "best." In that regard, his competitive nature is a plus in rehab! He is learning to take steps backwards (much harder for him at this point), has practiced climbing a four-inch step for the first time (up and backwards down, three times), and blew me away demonstrating how he could get off a bed, kneel on the ground, and then get back into the bed during one of his toughest physical therapy sessions. His therapist said, "Do NOT try this at home (yet)"...ha ha.

Fridays have become "go into the office day." For the last few weeks, he's gone into the office for at least three hours to catch up with briefs and to meet with his senior staff. That's been good for him (he calls these visits his "proof of life" visits for his staff), but I like them too because I can drop him off and relax with a coffee or run errands for a bit ;-)

We've found a handrail at the Regional Legal Service Office right across the street from us, where he's been standing, practicing lateral leg movements, lifting himself (with his legs and trying to get away from everything being primarily driven by his upper body), and doing controlled "sitting" back down—something he has improved at over the last few weeks. He jokes that there is a security camera near the handrails he uses—and is certain that someone will have quite the chuckle when they review the tapes!

We hosted another aviation leadership event this week—this time, for future commanding officers during their training pipeline. Typically, we host these monthly at our quarters, but until he's able to get into "the big house" as our grandson calls it, the director of the National Naval Aviation Museum was kind enough to open the doors after hours for a great mentoring event. Good to see him doing what he loves to do—talking about leadership and command to young commanders headed to their first squadron command.

[Note from Kyle]: This week was also special because Amy served as the honored guest speaker at the Pensacola Navy League's Military Spouse Appreciation Luncheon. For those who know Amy, although she's a brilliant hostess and can "talk the bark off a tree" in any sort of social setting, she is NOT a fan of public speaking. Well—after her remarks and, from what I understand, many teary eyes in the audience, her standing ovation probably means she'll be doing this again a time or two in the future. This was a team effort with some coaching along the way, but everyone in the audience really appreciated her personal stories of what it means to her to be a resilient and tough Navy spouse. After the last few months, I can't think of a better role model to demonstrate how special our military spouses are—and what they contribute to a military marriage.

Team Cozad continues to be positive, upbeat, and thankful for all the blessings in our lives.

———◇———

CHAPTER 17

Good Enough Is Never "Good Enough"

Our greatest weakness lies in giving up. The most certain way to succeed is always to try just one more time.

—Thomas Edison

Since those first few weeks at home, our new normal had continued to expand. As I mentioned, Amy and I took the advice of numerous counselors and therapists who recommended that, during the first two weeks, we limit our visitors to family. In retrospect, that 200-person party probably shattered the good advice that many smart people had given us into a million pieces. However, they told us to focus on what we needed to do and on establishing our routine, as it now included various articles of hospital equipment, wheelchairs, and limited mobility. Really limiting the visitors during those first few weeks (aside from that one event) allowed Amy and I to figure out what we needed to do every day. More importantly, it enabled us to learn how long it would take us to do those things and gave us an opportunity to adapt to our new living arrangements.

Now don't get me wrong—I had everything I needed in the small suite that others had prepared for me when I returned home for the first time. I had a comfortable bed (as comfortable as a temporary hospital bed could be), a TV, a full bathroom with a shower, and a work computer. It would have been easy to settle in, accept the progress we had made up to that point, and watch fifteen hours of television every day. But that's not how I roll. I refused to accept that there were some things that I just couldn't do. It didn't take long for me to start looking for those other things I could begin doing, such as more occupational-therapy-oriented activities.

It's funny how people find motivation to do what life requires of them. In all honesty, I didn't need much more motivation than just the thought of getting back into our house and sleeping in my own bed again. But that was one of those long-term goals. Getting back up to the second floor of Quarters A required several shorter-term accomplishments along the way.

My physical therapist knew the challenge of getting back into what my grandson calls the "big house." For starters, I would need to climb ten steps. I know that sounds easy, but for me, the thought of conquering ten steps felt almost as intimidating as thinking about climbing Mount Everest, and I'd have to make that climb every time I wanted to enter the house.

So, to achieve my initial ascent of the stairs, I had to set some interim short-term goals. My first short-term goal required working on leg strength and increasing my step height before beginning any stair work. It started by simply lifting my feet in alternating steps up and down a three-inch step while supporting myself between parallel bars. Soon, I increased to a five-inch step. Throughout my recovery, it motivated me to see measurable improvements in my physical abilities, and this one was literally my next step toward getting back into the house. With each effort, I could literally feel myself getting stronger and stronger.

The next challenge involved applying what I'd learned to do on level ground to real steps. We have five different sets of stairs that lead into the house at various entry points. After a quick survey, we decided that since I still had a pronounced lean forward when I stood up—primarily due to my lacking balance—one of our back stairways with a sturdy, open handrail provided the safest, sturdiest entry point on which to set our sights. With that in mind, we started climbing similar practice steps at West Florida during my physical therapy sessions. We developed an incremental plan of attack beginning with a three-inch step height. I'd go up all five steps, then back down. Exhausting, but I could do it without much assistance at all. After another therapy lesson, the time came to tackle the five-inch steps. Once again, I was out of breath by the time I had climbed up and back down, but I'd made encouraging progress. Unfortunately, I had to double that effort to get into the house, and as life would have it, the steps into our historical home rose two inches taller than the five-inch steps I trained on at therapy.

Luckily, I had some other inspiration to help accelerate my progress. Amy had fallen into the habit of talking about the house and the master bedroom as hers. I teased her that my name was still on the lease, and while she wasn't referring to the house as hers with any specific purpose, it had just become natural. After all, my man cave pretty much had everything I needed, right? I figured that the only way to stop her from talking about her house was to get myself back in.

In addition to having a strong desire to regain at least partial ownership in Quarters A, I was motivated by the fact that Amy and my therapist had given me a specific timeline on which to build the strength, coordination, and endurance to get back into the house. My therapist always presented things in terms of weeks. She had lined up exercises with more and more steps and balance drills that she thought would deliver my ability to safely climb the stairs in a month. Add another month, and that would convince her I could navigate my way up the additional twenty-three stairs to *our* master bedroom. (Notice, I emphasized "our" master bedroom!)

Well, Amy had another timeline. She wanted me back in the house by the Fourth of July and up in the bedroom by her birthday at the end of the same month. If you recall, I consider myself a pretty competitive guy. For competitive people, deadlines and records are meant to be beaten. Similarly, personal records are meant to be broken and improved upon. So, the challenge lay before me.

By mid-June, I could practice and ultimately defeat all ten steps on an indoor set of concrete stairs, each nearly eight inches tall, on the interior fire escape of West Florida. Like my previous attempts on smaller stairs, I was physically exhausted after one set of going up and then down again, but once you climbed up the ten steps at therapy, they didn't offer a quit option. You always had to climb back down.

In my mind, I had already conquered my Mount Everest. I now had the strength to go up and down in one single effort. The good news is, once I got up the stairs at the house, I had plenty of time to sit, enjoy being back in our home, and rest up for the journey back down. I intended to spend plenty of time enjoying being back in the house every time I made my ascent.

So, I felt ready to give it a shot. Due to this momentous occasion, and since we had a safety component to climbing those steps without my trained therapist there with us, we invited good friends over for the initial summit attempt. It ended up being easier than I had imagined, and before I knew it, I had made my return to the entertaining level of our quarters. Man, that first time getting back into the house really made me feel like I had just won the lottery. And just so you know, I made it up there almost two weeks ahead of schedule. Maybe there's something positive to be said about having a competitive attitude?

Now, the next twenty-three steps to our bedroom provided a bit more of a unique challenge. I knew that the banister didn't really offer the same support—way too low to provide the safety and stability that I'd need to get up to our living area. So, my next challenge was to figure out how I'd overcome that set of stairs.

At our next therapy session, we worked on various climbing techniques. I tried climbing up on my hands and knees, but it was terribly uncomfortable. So, we tried scooting up on my butt. I had strong enough thighs to push up to each next step and strong enough arms to lift my body onto the next level. This didn't seem so hard. But I had one other obstacle to overcome—getting from my wheelchair to the steps where I could start my scoot up.

During our next therapy day, the lightbulb came on for me. I guess you could say that many of my little progressions really depended on physical strength, stamina, and coordination. However, there is also a creative aspect to figuring out how to compensate for the things your body won't let you do. So, the overall key to progress really revolves around that combination of physical strength, stamina, and coordination mixed with imaginative problem-solving.

That day, only one short week after mastering those first ten steps, I figured out how to make that transfer from my wheelchair to the first of those next twenty-three steps. Get out of my way, I thought, because I'd had enough of sleeping in a man cave and desperately wanted to get back up to join Amy in "her" bedroom.

Now, Amy tends to be conservative and cautious when it comes to trying new things at home. Thankfully, when I learn new skills—or tricks, as I call them—if they are at all dicey, my physical therapist will quickly tell us, "Don't try this at home... yet." Since I didn't have that warning, I was ready to go. The good thing was that, unlike Mount Everest, I didn't need special climbing gear or even a Sherpa to make this climb.

So, nearly a month before Amy's birthday, I told her I wanted to practice making that transfer from my chair to the stairs but said I wouldn't climb the stairs because she was still a bit apprehensive about the whole thing. Every now and then, there is no harm in a little white lie.

As soon as I had transferred from my wheelchair to the stairs for the first time at home, I told her that since I'd accomplished that, I might as well try a step or two. Two turned into ten. Ten turned into twenty-three. And with our two yellow Labradors by my side every step of the way, I reached the summit. Up on the second floor, I had sight of our master bedroom.

Had I reached the apex of Mount Everest, I would have planted my flag, but at this point, I simply found contentment with never sleeping in that man cave again. I had some pride that I hadn't even required the use of an oxygen bottle or a Sherpa like those Mount Everest climbers typically rely on. I'd just leveraged that magical combination of creative problem-solving, endurance, one little white lie, and the relentless positivity that had become my hallmark.

Consider the significance of that day: In just over three months since my surgery, I'd returned to my house and figured out how to get up to our massive second floor. Mount Everest was nothing—I was on the second floor!

For the record, I broke the goal that Amy and my therapy team had set for me. As you can imagine, I was pumped knowing I had beat the record, and Amy just might have shed a few more happy tears that night.

It's Been a While...
Caring Bridge Journal Entry by Amy Cozad — June 23, 2018

Yes, it's been a while, and we originally thought slowing down on the updates made sense so we weren't spamming each week. But as we started putting this together, it's been a pretty incredible few weeks.

Kyle continues to gain strength and endurance on the walker. Although he tells everyone he's not ready to go "solo" at work or in the grocery store on his walker, he has upped his game to eighty yards in one effort. Add on top of that his therapy team has him working on going up/down curbs (no small feat with a walker), and the progress is noteworthy.

He's also mastering curbs in his wheelchair, which means he gets "wheelie" training...talk about a kid in a candy store! He said that was the most fun he's had yet!

We're regularly getting out of the house—dinner dates, work in the office every Friday, happy hour (Flight Suit Friday, of course), a recent visit by the Vice Chief of Naval Operations, and hosting a monthly social for our Navy's newest future commanding officers. We're actually planning our first overnight trip—one to Fort Walton Beach for a change of command and the second to Memphis to visit two of his commands (of course, that also means seeing the girls and our little grandson, Jaxon!)

Through our Navy caseworkers, we found out that Kyle qualifies as a wounded warrior under the Navy's Safe Harbor program. The Navy has done an incredible job taking care of Kyle and of those with similar injuries, and he's interested in helping to mentor others who are going through what he's been through as a way of giving back.

We had his three-month follow-up appointment this week with his neurosurgeon. This is the second time he's seen Kyle since the original surgery in March. More x-rays to assess the progress of his bone fusion with his titanium "hardware" and see how the healing process is progressing. And the great news: He's no longer required to wear his torso shell! Tonight was his "shell no!" debut at the Mustin Beach Officers Club, and although he's now using more core and back muscles to do what the shell did (posture and back stability), the little extra sore muscles he felt was worth the ice pack on his back when we got home! And, with our heat index over 100 degrees for the past few days, having that shell and extra undershirt gone from the mandatory wardrobe is SO much more comfortable!

Last but not least—his latest "trick," as he calls them, has been working on climbing stairs...yes, climbing stairs. With an open to below handrail (no wall behind), he can balance while getting both feet on each step and working his way up. Today— just over three months from his fall—he climbed our back steps and entered the house again for the first time since March 16th! I had asked him to work on that for my birthday in July, and in what he calls his "#CozadStrong" fashion and his no-quit approach to his recovery, he accomplished this incredible milestone over a month early!

We continue to be blessed with an incredible prayer and support network that extends from our Navy to local Pensacola to our extended national "family." We're not sure where his recovery will take us, but we wake up every morning looking forward to what we might be able to accomplish together! "Shell No!"

———◇———

"On the Road Again"
Caring Bridge Journal Entry by Amy Cozad — July 24, 2018

So, it's been a few weeks, but once again—some big things to pass along. I caught myself telling Kyle that "this is all moving too fast...you're making progress faster than I can process." Is that ironic, or what?

As soon as we came home from the hospital, I told Kyle that I had one goal—to get him into the house before my birthday this month. At that point, I hadn't given much thought to getting him upstairs and back sleeping in OUR bed. Now, for perspective, the ten steps that he now climbs every day just to get to the ground level of our home is just the start. Our therapist came up with a plan that she promised would have him scooting up the remaining twenty-three steps (yes, twenty-three... that's not a TYPO) by the end of August. Well, overachiever that he is—after just a week of the exercises that she had set up for him, he climbed all twenty-three steps and is now a "full-time" resident in our house again. It's not easy, but as he tells me all the time—"I'm a sailor, and sailors are tough. There's no easy road to recovery." Yes, I had tears in my eyes the first night he was able to get upstairs.

And about his walker...he's been using it around the house more—really using it to navigate those places where his chair won't fit. Anyway, as he keeps getting stronger, his steps increase. Today, he walked as well as I've ever seen—small steps but with good control of his feet: toes pointed straight ahead and stronger than I've seen. At the end, his therapist commented on how many feet he'd just walked. She was quickly corrected when Kyle said, "110 yards sounds MUCH better than 330 feet." No—he's not lost his competitive spirit.

And as we continue to expand the definition of our new normal, we both went to Fort Walton Beach, FL, where he presided over a change of command ceremony for one of his commanding officers two weeks ago. We ventured out on a manageable drive (two hours with traffic), and before the ceremony, he got to tour the Navy's dive school and meet with his Commanding Officer/Executive Officer and Command Master Chief teams. Then, he was honored to participate in a master dive qualification pinning ceremony (as if getting back out to one of his schools wasn't enough!) That night also marked another first for us—we stayed in a place that didn't end in "hospital." We stayed in Destin, FL, had a great dinner at the hotel's five-star restaurant, and expanded the list of "firsts."

And that stay in Destin was a good "warmup," as he committed to attend another change of command and spend two days with other direct report commanders in Millington, TN. He did great with the seven-hour drive (his back is getting stronger and stronger), so now he's talking about flying...I'm not ready for that! For the first time, I left him with his aide and force master chief (thanks, guys) who took him from meeting to meeting and brought him back to the hotel. On the second day, I went to see my parents, and when I returned to the hotel, he had come in through the lobby, ridden the elevator, let himself into our room, and managed to change from his uniform to a set of shorts and a shirt and was making work calls when I returned. Okay, his calls were complete and he just might have been napping...At any rate, it's getting hard to hold him back.

One final funny story since our sense of humor continues to be an important part of our daily "therapy." We were able to see our three-year-old grandson who really has an incredible sense of what his "poppa" is going through. Whenever we were out (he loves to ride in Kyle's lap and wants to do wheelies whenever I'll let them), he made it a point to explain to anyone who walked within earshot that "my poppa's got an 'owwie' on his back." How is that for a sympathetic kid? Well—mostly sympathetic. You see, Kyle had his walker out in our room and challenged Jaxon to a race. As Kyle stepped out across the room, Jaxon looked back at me and commented, "Poppa is slowwwww." Ah, from the mouths of babes!

At any rate, just prior to my birthday, with Kyle in the house again, he and I continue to feel blessed with everything we've been able to accomplish as a team. The "Team Cozad" concept isn't one that is new to us throughout our years of service—but the manner in which we apply it every single day is new. We continue to be amazed at the love and support we get from our family, our close friends, and our Navy family and from an incredible therapy team that pushes him to new levels every week.

CHAPTER 18

Living with Purpose

People are always blaming circumstances for what they are.
I don't believe in circumstances. The people who get ahead
in this world are the people who get up and look for
the circumstances they want, and if they can't
find them, make them.

—George Bernard Shaw

Still to this day, when I see old acquaintances, work colleagues, and other friends for the first time since my accident, I tend to get a standard response: "You look much better than I thought you would." I never know how to take that because I'm not sure what people expect me to look like. With the exception of that pesky paralysis that has taken my lower body, I feel great. I feel strong, and in many cases, despite the wheelchair, I'm quite certain that nobody would know I've suffered an injury like the one I did. I'm never sure if folks expected me to look like I lay at death's front door, or if they expected me to have IV machines taped to my arms while wearing a hospital gown twenty-four hours a day, every day of the week. Well, that's not the case. That's just not me.

So, the next question I get is: "You look great. Why do you think that is?" That's both an interesting and introspective question, but I attribute that perception of looking normal to a few things. I've already described the importance a support network plays in helping someone maintain the relentless positivity required during a long-term recovery. For me, having someone with the strength and unselfishness that Amy has demonstrated each and every day rests at the top of my list. But there are other aspects of my recovery, second only to her support.

The other thing that's really helped me maintain a focus on recovery while staying optimistic has been what I'll call in generic terms my purpose. Having some defined sense of purpose served as my motivation to get out of my hospital bed, get away from the TV, and channel any excess energy into something meaningful. That purpose helped me to continue with my recovery and keep setting my goals higher and higher each week. For me, that meaningful purpose pushed me back into working as a naval officer and attempting to make that comeback that Charles Krauthammer described. For me, one of those clear purposes and bases for my comeback focused on resuming my full-time role as commander of the Naval Education and Training Command.

In naval service, the more senior one becomes, they typically move further away from doing what they love to do and what attracted them to service in the first place—in my case, flying. I really loved to fly but accepted the fact that the more senior I became, the fewer opportunities I'd have to fly. That's okay because, for me, the tradeoff presented a greater opportunity to lead some great American servicemen and -women. Although my later assignments took me away from flight time, I was still in the thick of training and leading young sailors and officers.

At the time of my accident, I commanded the Navy's largest shore command—the Naval Education and Training Command, or NETC in the Navy's love for acronyms, with over 50,000 servicemen, servicewomen, and civilians responsible for the Navy's street to fleet accession training process. That process accounts for the time and methods by which we recruit men and women to serve, then train them within our boot camp, where in just eight short weeks, we transform young civilians into capable sailors. At that point, those new sailors go through their initial technical training before we send them to their first ship, squadron, submarine, or platoon in the fleet.

There is nothing more energizing than watching our next generation eager to join the Navy and become a part of an organization that is greater than the sum of its individuals. The one thing that rivals the energy of our newest recruits and new sailors is the dedication of our recruiters, recruit division commanders, and technical instructors that take them from civilian to sailor. I did miss flying and instructing but can think of few places I would have rather served at the time of my accident. That place provided the inspiration and motivation for me to recover and improve each and every day.

Now, first things first. In my decades of serving, I've always pushed myself hard to perform at a high level. In retrospect, I've experienced times when I've lost focus on which priorities I valued as most important. But one thing I saw with clarity while still in the ICU was that, going forward, my family and health had to be the first priority. My injury really served to help me reassess my work-life balance, regardless of what my future held.

As a starting point, during my time in the ICU and during

my inpatient hospital stay, I completely detached from my job. No meetings. No phone calls. No computer and, therefore, no emails. For a driven, perfectionist leader who had commanded on five different occasions during the previous three decades, I found it much easier to do than I would have ever imagined. Well, I'm sure that painkillers initially made that easier than I would have previously thought, but it helped reinforce that the time had come to focus first and foremost on my health and recovery.

Yes, it's easy to say that life presents a balancing act of competing priorities for us to manage, but it's harder to translate those words into actions. It doesn't matter what line of work you are in. Some people manage those priorities much better than others, and I was probably somewhere in the middle. Prior to my injury, I had always thought of myself as a devoted father and husband, but over thirty years of service in the Navy certainly influenced how successfully I balanced all those priorities.

Yes, I'm talking about that work-life balance challenge. As one becomes more senior in their respective profession, the specific leadership roles and demands that come with that responsibility often manifest themselves in long hours, frequent travel, and work that sometimes finds its way home on the weekends. That's not to say that senior officers love their families any less, but some are more effective at finding ways to keep that balance in check and not allow work to become life's only focus.

Following my injury, I had some help to keep me in the right mind, to focus on the right things, and to ensure I had my priorities in the right place. I like to think that I'm the one who made it clear to my bosses—both my Navy boss and my most important boss, Amy—that recovery was my number one priority. Those five weeks of cold turkey following my accident forced me to delegate everything to my staff in the day-to-day business of naval education and training. Once again, it's fair to assume that my painkillers helped in that effort, but frankly, I had a lot of assistance making sure that I concentrated on my recovery, my health, and my family, first and foremost.

One of the key elements that helped with my prioritization came from the support I received from my Navy chain of command. They made it clear within the first week of my hospitalization that I had the support of my entire Navy family. From our Chief of Naval Operations to my immediate boss the Chief of Naval Personnel, Navy leaders at the highest levels demonstrated that getting back into my job came secondary to my health. They told me to focus on the important things—on mending my body and on that full recovery that everyone really wanted me to achieve. That incredibly powerful message meant so much to me. I'd seen that same support for other peers who had gone through chemo treatments for cancer or other significant hospitalizations, but it was now personal. It wasn't lip service, and it really proved to me that, regardless of the size of our corporate Navy, they made the people who breathed life into our service top priority.

In that regard, it's a blessing to serve in an organization that clearly put me, the person, before work and the job. When you consider the magnitude of that statement, it's pretty profound. An organization like the Navy thrives on competition while building the readiness to project power, to deter conflict, and in those rare cases when that's not enough, to decisively defeat any adversary under any terms. We don't often see the compassionate side of the Navy, which unquestionably put my recovery, and its impact on my family, at the top of their priorities. From that first day waking up in the ICU, I've noticed the same focus over and over again, and I know that approach is not unique to me or to only the most senior officers. The Navy's approach to recovery and rehabilitation supporting those seriously wounded, ill, or injured runs deep in commitment, regardless of rank.

Once I had returned home, I made Amy a promise. I would never miss a physical therapy appointment during the week, making that my highest priority. Having made that commitment, I began the process of inching my way back into my work routine. Clearly, I couldn't jump in on a full-time basis, but with a work computer and work iPad in my temporary quarters, I could start to ease my way back in, even if only teleworking with my staff on major issues.

Since mastering the stairs in our house, I continued to increase my work routine on a "not to interfere" basis with physical therapy. I scheduled everything around physical therapy on Mondays, Tuesdays, and Thursdays. If I had an important meeting on the schedule with my boss, I delegated that to my highly capable front office staff. Physical therapy continued to be the predominant factor influencing how far I progressed, so that remained my first priority.

Balancing work and life, whether specific to family or health, isn't something that comes naturally to many senior business executives or senior military officers. Having said that, it's not hard for me to understand that some senior leaders assume that it is unrealistic to be successful at a very high executive level while effectively balancing the seemingly competing demands at work and home. In pursuing that better balance between work, family, and recovery, I was able to pursue that sense of purpose I realized was so important in encouraging and motivating me to continue in my rehabilitation.

I started that portion of my comeback by going into my office one day each week. I enjoyed seeing my staff and, in a subtle way, demonstrating to them that my accident wouldn't stop me from practicing as much normality as possible. My routine became more comfortable and my ability to manage more and more within my new normal expanded over the next few months. As I gained strength, I pushed my envelope from emails, phone calls, and staff meetings at my house to getting into my office as my endurance allowed. At first, I joked with my staff that I needed to start doing "proof of life" visits so the staff knew that there really was a person on the other end of the phone line or email. I also teased them that I had to make sure that, in my medical absence, someone hadn't taken my roster photograph off the command photo board or removed me as the commander.

Over time, I continued to incrementally become more and more active at work. Much of my routine involved teleworking from the house through phone-in meetings, emails, and staff meetings in my small room. Although I had a bit of an unconventional schedule, I considered myself back in full swing at work. I did have to compensate my work hours to offset the twelve or so hours each week when I was off at physical therapy. Typically, I would catch up from the house at night or during quiet Saturday or Sunday mornings. Not ideal, but a small price to pay for the privilege of commanding the Navy's largest shore command. I figured if President Franklin Delano Roosevelt could run a country while confined to a wheelchair, I could spend an hour or two working during the weekends so I could continue to do the job I love, right?

As Amy and I continued to stretch the definition of our new normal, we didn't limit that to getting back into my work routine. Within a few months, we had our first overnight in a hotel, our first trip out of town (that one in a car), and, ultimately, my first few Navy trips in which we tested our ability to tackle airports, security checkpoints, and airline travel. It might not sound too significant to someone who wasn't aware of my story, but in less than six months, I was back in full force at work. Of course, because of my ongoing physical therapy appointments, I had to balance any travel around that commitment.

When different commands asked me to deliver graduation remarks for our Navy's Officer Candidate School and Recruit Training Command, I worked hard in physical therapy so that I could stand from my wheelchair. Climbing the stairs in Quarters A might have felt like I had just conquered Mount Everest, but standing to deliver congratulations and words of encouragement to our Navy's newest ensigns and sailors felt like I had just landed on the moon. Hard work certainly paid off, and with these new firsts, I really began to feel back in my game.

CHAPTER 19

Wounded Warrior

*Most of the important things in the world have
been accomplished by people who have kept on trying
when there seemed to be no hope at all.*

—Dale Carnegie

In addition to my family and my desire to get back into my
job routine, I discovered another area that has really helped me
focus on my purpose going forward and has been incredibly
important in allowing me to keep the optimistic outlook I've
maintained throughout my recovery. As I worked through my
"Why me?" stage in the ICU, I quickly transitioned to a stage
where I grew to accept my injury, my paralysis, and what it
meant. Of course, I did so under the continuing belief that I
would walk again one day. Although I didn't understand why,
God had chosen to put me on a new and different path that no
one had expected. Through my faith, I accepted the fact that,
although I didn't understand why, there was a higher purpose.

Within days of being discharged from West Florida
Rehabilitation Center, I received a call from the local Navy Safe

Harbor office requesting a visit from my newly assigned case-worker. I had heard of the Navy Safe Harbor program, but like a majority of my Navy peers, I had little understanding of what they really did. Actually, I had no idea. So, I Googled them. According to their website, the "Navy Wounded Warrior–Safe Harbor is the Navy's sole organization for coordinating the non-medical care of seriously wounded, ill, and injured sailors providing resources and support to their families." Hmmm. Wounded warrior? I assumed they were two different but related programs. During the first visit with my caseworker, she informed me that, based on the severity of my injury, not only had I qualified as a Navy wounded warrior, but I was likely the most senior wounded warrior on active duty in our service.

I'm sure I wasn't unique in my thinking that wounded warriors were all victims of combat-related injuries. During that first meeting with my local caseworker, she relayed that, when they initially established the program, they solely focused on care and support for those who had suffered combat-related injuries. Within two years of inception, the program had expanded to include all personnel who were wounded and seriously ill or injured when that illness or injury had occurred while they were on active duty. So, the program registered me as a category three wounded warrior, the highest characterization based on the severity of my injury. Wounded warrior. What an unlikely outcome.

To tell you the truth, I really didn't care what anyone called me. The fact remained that I had suffered a significant injury that would require months, if not years, of therapy to achieve the level of recovery that I had in mind. The more I learned, the more interested I became, and I thought about others like me—folks who had been injured in the line of duty or people severely ill and hospitalized. *There might be an opportunity here*, I thought. I was living proof that injury and illness can and do happen to anyone. They don't discriminate based on race or gender, and my case proved that they don't discriminate based on rank. The more I thought about the program and what it does for servicemen and -women, the more I thought that I might have found a new calling and certainly another sense of purpose for which I was uniquely qualified.

Back to my earlier comment about God's purpose. Throughout my recovery—when in the ICU, while admitted as a patient at West Florida for my initial month of intensive physical therapy, and even after they discharged me—I have been described as many things, but one stands out and has to deal with what one good friend described as my relentless positivity. It wasn't uncommon to have similar questions from friends: How do you remain so positive, so optimistic, given your original medical prognosis? How do you remain so focused and confident in your ability to make a full recovery?

It wasn't until I learned about Navy Safe Harbor and my wounded warrior status that I started to come to terms with why I might have been put in my specific new place in life. Dictated only by circumstances, I had a unique position to mentor others who had suffered similar catastrophic injuries—not because of my rank or seniority but based on my personal experience. My position gave me the opportunity and, I guess, a platform from which to advocate and create awareness on the policies and programs that impacted other wounded warriors like myself.

It wasn't long before I made connections with others who found themselves hospitalized with injuries that would require months of therapy on their individual roads to recovery. And it wasn't long before I embraced that sense of purpose, having a chance to talk to others and to provide common stories of encouragement that I'd learned firsthand during my recovery. I began to help educate others on the programs, benefits, and policies that I'd discovered through the help of Navy Safe Harbor–Wounded Warrior or through my own personal research. Frankly, I get as much motivation and encouragement from sharing stories with others who are going through exactly the same rehabilitation program as I probably provide for them.

In doing this, I discovered that an institutional mutual support network wasn't readily available. As I've said before, the opportunity to talk person to person with someone who's "been there, done that" is an important part of any recovery. As odd as it might sound, that initial unwanted notification of "Sir, based on the severity of your injury, you qualify for enrollment in the Wounded Warrior program" quickly became the likely reason and maybe the purpose for which I'd been searching.

CHAPTER 20

It's Alright Not to Be Alright

*Permanence, perseverance, and persistence in spite of
all obstacles, discouragements, and impossibilities: It is this,
that in all things distinguishes the strong soul from the weak.*

—Thomas Carlyle

When we first moved to Pensacola, part of getting settled into the community included finding a church that we liked and fit into. We tried a few, and as nice as they were, we couldn't find that perfect match. Following a recommendation from a reliable source, we decided to try an otherwise unlikely worship service venue.

I can vividly remember when I was a student in flight school and others suggested "go-to" places in Pensacola for a young naval aviator to frequent on any night of the week for a fun time. Many recommended a shabby beach joint called the Flora-Bama. I best remember the Flora-Bama as an amazing night spot on the world's whitest beaches in Perdido Key.

The club was known for having live bands and the world's best Bushwacker drinks as well as for hosting a legendary annual mullet toss contest to which thousands flocked each year.

When our good friends mentioned that the Flora-Bama hosted a worship service on Sundays, based on my only recollection, Amy and I hesitated. Well, we didn't give it a second thought when another good friend mentioned the same and guaranteed us that we would certainly enjoy the service and the pastor's uncanny ability to deliver a weekly message that resonated with everyone. So, I talked Amy into going one Sunday, and the church delivered. The venue looked far from traditional with the makeshift worship hall transformed from the live entertainment stage and dance floor from the night before. We found the pastor, the people, and the message incredible. We enjoyed the sermon and really liked the diversity of the congregation.

The congregation's motto struck me first thing. Posters on the wall, handouts for the hymns and bible readings, and all the ushers' T-shirts were proudly adorned with the phrase, "It's alright not to be alright." When you think about it, that's a cool message for a church. No one is perfect, and we all need to acknowledge that we all fall short of perfection in our daily pursuit of being better people. It's alright not to be alright.

After my injury, that motto took on a different meaning for me. It's alright not to be alright. Now that I consistently dealt with a wheelchair, those initial days of getting out in public or even just going into work felt awkward. I knew that I was still the same person that I'd been before my accident, but the simple fact that I was in a wheelchair couldn't be ignored.

Technically, hundreds of thousands of Americans are disabled just as I am. Handicapped. I certainly never thought of myself as handicapped even after finding myself dependent on a wheelchair for mobility. Maybe that's part of the reason that I've maintained an optimistic attitude and that relentless positivity during my recovery.

Nonetheless, it was still hard for me to get back into any public setting during those initial months of being at home. I guess the way I looked at things, I used to see anyone with a handicap and have a sympathetic eye toward their hardship. I now had a much different view since I lived among that hand-icapped population. I didn't want anyone feeling sorry for me or showing sympathy. I wanted them to get out of my way so I could do my job.

In addition to Charles Krauthammer's example and the quote that really encouraged me to push myself during my hos-pitalization, another person served as an inspiration to me. I mentioned earlier that if President Franklin Delano Roosevelt could run an entire country from his wheelchair, then surely I could resume my role as commander of the Naval Education and Training Command. Part of that belief centered on the fact that I refused to take no for an answer. Well, for the most part. That climb to the crest of Mount Everest, as I called my ascent up our stairs to my bedroom, might have taken me a few weeks longer than I wanted to achieve, but I viewed everything else as being within my grasp with a little hard work, creativity, and perseverance.

One thing that I wanted to make sure I did differently from FDR centered on how he and others managed his persona in the eye of the public. I researched and found it difficult to find pictures of FDR in his wheelchair. Most of what I found would hide his chair behind a desk or would only show his head and shoulders in an attempt to make him appear just like every other guy. Some had the opinion that the President's public image would be diminished if others associated him with a known handicap. Others concluded that the lack of public acknowledgement resulted from an intentional effort to protect FDR's privacy. Regardless, it felt to me that a public bias existed that didn't readily accept that the President's handicap had absolutely nothing to do with his ability to lead our country and to impose a national strategy during a critical time in our nation's history.

So, I made an intentional effort to build the confidence to spend time in public. As I understand it now, there is a perceived human bias that tends to look at someone with a disability a little differently than we look at everyone else. As a result, just getting out of the house during our first visits to local restaurants or social get-togethers made me uncomfortable. I felt as if everyone stared at me. I was different now, and I had complete awareness of that difference. As the senior Navy officer in Pensacola, I was a pretty recognizable figure, and that just seemed to amplify my perceptions.

With time, I embraced the fact that I wasn't unique. There are literally hundreds of thousands of people in our country who are confined to wheelchairs or who depend on walkers, canes, or crutches for their mobility. So, as they say, practice makes perfect, and with greater frequency, increasing confidence, and an undeniable bout with humility, I quickly powered through the awkward stage of getting back out in public. The more I did it, the more comfortable I felt. Your new normal won't ever be normal until you get yourself out there. Ultimately, I was so successful at overcoming that reluctance that Amy had to struggle to keep me at home.

As I became stronger and gained more confidence in getting out in public, I wanted to overcome the image of FDR and any perception of an appearance of trying to hide my temporary handicap. Whether I was going to dinner with Amy in town, going into work and wheeling around the headquarters to say hello to my staff, or traveling and participating in other official military duties, I made a conscious effort to get back to a similar level of engagement that helped define me prior to my injury. That meant doing unconventional things and different things from what folks in uniform normally saw. I mean, how many sailors are used to seeing a two-star admiral wheeling around their schoolhouse or an ordinance disposal range in a wheelchair? How many are used to seeing a guest speaker with tons of gold stripes on his uniform rolling his wheelchair up a handicap ramp or onto an elevator to speak at a military graduation?

As I started getting back in this otherwise familiar routine, I kept falling back to the phrase I first heard at the Flora-Bama. It's alright not to be alright. Heck, I felt alright but fully acknowledged the fact that, to others, I might look just a bit different from other senior officers in our military. However, I wouldn't allow that to interfere with what I needed to do.

With that growing confidence, I actively looked for opportunities to venture out and interact in a variety of social and professional settings. I accepted guest speaking roles at various venues, including the Navy's Recruit Training Command graduation where we recognized nearly 900 of our Navy's newest sailors ready to join the fleet. I traveled to Newport, Rhode Island, to officiate the graduation and commissioning ceremony at our Officer Candidate School, similarly recognizing the accomplishments of eighty new ensigns to our Navy.

Eventually, that initial difficulty in traveling about and assuming my previous normal role all but vanished. Having said that, my confidence did come with a realization that people did look at me differently. I came to embrace the opportunity that I'd been given. I wanted people to see that I'm still the same guy. I'm still the same leader. Still the same husband, dad, and grandfather. After all, I'm the same person I've always been. I'm just a bit slower and shorter when I'm in my wheelchair.

I've gotten used to joining a part of the large number of handicapped Americans today who depend on wheelchairs for their mobility. That aside, to my knowledge, I was the only flag officer in the United States Navy who's in that same position. I teased my staff at the time that, although your boss looks different now, I'm not. It's the same old me, so get used to it. Part of achieving my new normal was overcoming the awkward stares, silence, and looks that I tended to get when I attended any official functions. But I'll admit, as I got back into the public speaking that goes with being a flag officer, I enjoyed the opportunity to talk to people. And I didn't shy away from telling my story. After all, I'd come to the conclusion that, given a variety of factors, I have a unique position to advocate for disability awareness to multiple audiences.

I made it a point to talk about this incredible opportunity the Navy had given me—an opportunity that I didn't take for granted. In a speech to a large military audience at the Newport Navy Ball in 2019, I made a point to speak about opportunity and how, as individuals, we need to embrace the opportunities that fate provides us in our lives.

After my injury, the Navy could have easily taken what many folks would argue was the easy way forward. That path could have resulted in my medical retirement, and as a result, identifying a suitable replacement in my current command position. Instead, the Navy granted me an opportunity. Since the accident only created one difference—my mobility—I remained fully qualified to do everything required for success in my job. They had given me the opportunity to continue to lead, despite what others consider a handicap. I still had a tremendous passion for the mission of recruiting and training our Navy's newest sailors and officers, and I had no intention of walking away from those duties. I was committed to making the whole thing work, from recovery to ongoing physical therapy to gradual reintroduction into a pretty rigorous work routine to the travel that went along with leading a training enterprise as large as the one under my responsibility.

Despite my injury, I still considered myself a progressive leader who understood what it took to effectively develop my subordinates and create an environment that supported necessary change. I also considered myself a strategic thinker who could communicate a mission vision at a high level while turning that strategy into actionable improvement to process and execution. I remained as competitive as I'd ever been and still maintained that Type A personality so instrumental to my ongoing recovery. In simple terms, my drive to lead an organization that produced at a top-tier level never wavered.

In fact, my staff used to tease me that I'm very much like the fictional movie character Ricky Bobby—a NASCAR knockoff who just wanted to go fast. That's an oversimplification, but I do want to go fast and lead the world's preeminent training command in delivering world-class training for our Navy. Slow and methodical doesn't deliver the agility, the high end of technology, or the quality of training we owe our sailors today.

Another component of re-immersing myself into the social and public aspect of operating as a two-star Navy admiral was the challenges and additional logistics involved in travel and public speaking after my accident. With that in mind, it's easy to point to the role my staff took immediately after my accident and as I continued with my treatment and return to work. They surveyed our headquarters building, originally built as the Pensacola base hospital in 1941 and used in that capacity until 1978. Needless to say, the old building wasn't necessarily handicapped friendly for today's standards, despite being a hospital. I think the ramp we initially used to get my wheelchair access had previously served as the roll-in/roll-out to the former hospital morgue, so every afternoon when I'd leave for the day, I'd smile as I exited, thinking, "I'm not going out that way today. I'll make it on my own power this time!"

When he first arrived, I used to tease my flag aide that he had the easiest job in the Navy because, during my hospital stay, I had no daily schedule to arrange and certainly no travel. However, as I became stronger and gained greater independence stepping back into my job, I changed my tone. At that point, he had the most complicated job in the Navy. He worried about wheelchair access. He worried about elevators and how I could get up and down to a speaking dais or stage. He concerned himself with podium heights and protocol details that aren't typically considerate of a boss like his. My aide even became an expert in examining venue photographs to determine how best to get me into a given building. He'd survey the slope of a given ramp, and most of the time, he was flawless. With his support, I returned to full swing. I used the "I'm different" refrain as an opportunity to help educate others in our Navy and in our communities about how each military service has committed itself to taking care of its wounded warriors like me.

As two hours of work a day turned into full days and eventually into travel, there is no doubt (and an equally huge sense of appreciation), based on my new mobility requirements, that my staff had inherited a tough job. I remember on my first trip back to Newport, Rhode Island, to visit some of our commands there, we arrived during a week of torrential rainstorms. With the pre-trip survey completed, said trusty aide had everything mapped out. Well, they say that any good war plan never survives first contact because the enemy gets a vote. That week, we found out that, in addition to the enemy, the weather gets a vote.

When we arrived at a flooded entry, a set of stairs provided the only alternative. Granted, there were only five or six stairs, but they were tough to navigate in my wheelchair. I think that trip officially graduated me from the "Geez, I feel awkward in public" phase of my recovery and transition back to work.

Without skipping a beat, I looked at the commanding officer, his executive officer, and the command master chief, all very senior guys with a sum of probably seventy-five years of serving between them, and said, "What are you guys waiting for? Haven't you ever picked up a wheelchair and carried it up these steps? Let's go, lads, hoist away. I'm speaking to your students in less than five minutes." And hoist away they did. In their defense, I'm certain that they had never hoisted a wheelchair at the Navy's Command Leadership School until that day. I guess we can put that one in the books for posterity's sake.

One final element of returning to my normal routine outside

of my physical therapy, my work, and my travel schedule was ensuring I still made room for the most important and enduring aspect of my life—spending quality time with Amy. She would argue that she gets too much time with me these days, but she'd say that in jest. Making sure she has time for herself, as well as quiet time where we can just talk about the things couples talk about, is important.

Amy, too, found value in me returning to work. When she initially dropped me off for my time in the office, she fondly referred to it as daddy daycare. She would smile and tell my staff, "He's all yours. I'll see you this afternoon!" Outside of daddy daycare, we had really become active getting out and enjoying all those great treasures that Pensacola and the panhandle of west Florida have to offer. Enjoying community events, taking walks with the dogs along the seawall near our house when I was strong enough to use a recumbent bike, and going on date nights made things continue to feel more normal.

Yes, in the months and now years following my accident, I've accepted the fact that I am different. Having said that, I've also achieved a level of independence and conquered new abilities to a point where I really don't think I'm *that* different. I've come to embrace the fact that we are all different—and it's alright not to be alright. Ultimately, I came to a profound realization that, based on the goals I set for myself in a return to full duty, I not only had a platform but I had things I wanted to prove to anyone who happened to be watching.

CHAPTER 21

#BeInspired

I will never quit...if knocked down, I will get up every time...
I will draw on every ounce of strength to protect my teammates
and to accomplish our mission. I am NEVER out of the fight.

—Excerpt from the U.S. Navy SEAL Ethos

Throughout my busy career, I've always been an active guy. Following a decent athletic career in high school and my time as a basketball player at the Naval Academy, I carried that active lifestyle forward after I graduated. I love the outdoors, hiking, camping, fishing, and other activities characteristic of an active adult. Considering the jobs I've had in my career, the Navy, and any of the other armed services, demands a level of physical fitness and has a culture founded on that type of activity. I can count on one hand the number of couch potatoes I've run across during my decades in uniform. Simply put, naval officers are typically driven go-getters who hate to sit around and wait for something to happen. Instead, we prefer to make things happen.

Several months after my release from the hospital, someone from the Navy Wounded Warrior office contacted me and asked if I had any interest in adaptive sports. Frankly, I had no idea what that meant, but their question intrigued me. Nine short months after waking up in a hospital to the news from my neurosurgeon that, based on the severity of the spinal cord injury, I would never get out of a wheelchair, I found myself headed to Naval Station Mayport, Florida to see just what this adaptive sports thing was all about.

To this day, I still find myself learning—learning how to overcome a physical barrier, learning how to get around places that are not wheelchair or handicapped friendly, and overcoming some of the preconceived notions that I still have to this day. Amy tells people that we've become complex problem solvers. In much simpler terms, I tell people that we just refuse to accept "no" and "can't" as a final answer. We just git 'er done, regardless of what that takes.

So, on our way to that very first adaptive sports camp, I had this vision that I'd work and play among a group of amputees and wheelchair veterans in a somewhat gentlemanly pace. I couldn't have been more incorrect in my assumption. Even though they described the camp as introductory, the coaches were dead serious. I signed up for recumbent biking, sitting volleyball, and rowing, since at one point or another in my previous able-bodied life, I'd had a chance to do each.

My fondest memory came from my introduction to sitting or seated volleyball. Almost exactly like the sport we watch on the Olympics, the biggest difference is that the adaptive version of the sport calls for a much lower net height (three feet and nine point two eight inches to be precise) and the players must keep their butts in contact with the ground at all times. Sounds simple, right? Not so much.

That first time I played, I introduced myself to the other camp adaptive athletes. Remember my assumption that I'd get to meet other folks with spinal cord injuries and prosthetic limbs? Nope. I overestimated that in a big way. Each of the other athletes appeared able-bodied. The Wounded Warrior program supports active duty servicemembers and veterans with a variety of serious illnesses or injuries. That could mean one person is battling cancer, another is working through post-traumatic stress disorder, and others have prosthetic limbs or limited mobility. As I wheeled myself out to the court and lifted myself from my chair to the ground, another dozen folks joined me, all walking normally, and for the life of me, I questioned, "Hmm, what's wrong with that dude? Am I in the right place?"

We went through a series of drills and eventually played a few practice matches just to introduce each of us newbies to this variation of the sport. For those who have never seen a sitting volleyball match, the player's ability to move around the court depends on a combination of movements with one's hands and feet. You push, you pull, and you scoot around to get to the ball. Thick, padded shorts are highly encouraged since you're dragging your backside across the hard-surfaced court, but the combination of using arms and feet to push, pull, and propel you around makes for one heck of a workout.

I quickly learned that, without the feeling or use of my feet, I required a combination pull and drag. I'd pull myself with my arms and upper body as I dragged my feet along behind. I proved that I was clearly not the quickest person on the court, and I discovered that the old Cozad drag move caused a surprising amount of skin abrasions on both ankles. When the coach had to stop play, it took me a minute to realize that those abrasions had streaked the court with my blood. Ah, the joys of not having any feeling to realize that I had bloodied both ankles. Coach decided to clean the court a bit and told everyone to go get a bottle of water across the gym.

That first water break still brings a smile to my face. In the blink of an eye, all the other athletes popped up and trotted across the gym. I sat there like a stranded turtle on the beach and shouted, "Can a brother get a little help over here?" Everyone laughed, and within a short time bonding on the sitting volleyball court, an instant friendship developed among previous strangers, many of whom went on to represent Team Navy in the 2019 Department of Defense Warrior Games in Tampa.

My recovery had transitioned to a place where I now looked for things to get me out there. I had returned to a modified full work schedule at this point. Amy would drop me off at the office each day and then pick me up each afternoon for our drive across town to attend outpatient physical therapy. Then, I'd finish my workday at home after everyone else on my staff had departed for the day. That's when I'd sort through the emails, briefs, and projects that I'd missed while at physical therapy.

When I was invited to attend the Navy's tryout camp for adapted athletes as they formed the Navy team that would ultimately represent our service at the Department of Defense Warrior Games later that summer, I jumped at the opportunity. I realized my unicorn status as certainly the only two-star admiral in our Navy working through a spinal cord injury, and without a doubt, the most senior and oldest athlete in the bunch. Trying to balance a return to work, continued rehabilitation and recovery, and now adaptive sports, I remained grateful to Navy leadership that gave me the chance (and a unique platform) to represent the Navy Wounded Warrior program in a way I hadn't really imagined.

The team tryouts made a lasting impression and opened my mind to many things that I'd not yet considered. I really didn't have an expectation that I'd make the team. After all, the others working to secure a spot on Team Navy were nearly half my age and in pretty darn good shape. Plus, I'd never played many of the sports that we'd compete for. Since doctors had only recently medically cleared me from wearing that composite protective shell, I couldn't compete in some of the contact sports like wheelchair basketball and rugby. So, I stuck to what I'd done in Mayport and practiced rowing and cycling, though I intentionally decided that seated volleyball definitely wasn't my sport. They also convinced me to participate in the field activities (discus and shot put) given my long arms, despite the fact that I had never thrown either of the implements in my life.

In addition to a full eight-hour practice schedule each day, we spent time together as a group. During those times, we got to know each other on a very personal basis. Despite being the oldest and most senior in the group, everyone agreed (some more reluctantly than others since they were so junior in their Navy service) to call me by my first name. Before we could gel as a team, we had to think and feel like a family. I also encouraged everyone to consider me just another member of the team. "Don't take it easy on me on the court or the road or the field." Big mistake on my part as these young whippersnappers were not shy about doing exactly that. No mistaking the fact that nobody took it easy on the old guy.

During those intense seven days, we all became friends. Given my age, many called me the silverback, referencing the silverback gorilla that typically stands out as the old man in a gorilla troop. During that week, the most common question we asked of one another was, "What's your story?" It became so natural and so refreshing to tell folks how my injury happened, the prognosis, and how I handled things, and others felt equally willing to share their stories and, in many cases, their vulnerabilities. From those conversations developed lifelong friendships and relationships based on common experience. Within our week together, we truly had become a family.

Now, I'm not going to lie. Remember me? Mr. Type A personality. Arrogant naval aviator. I wanted to be the best, and I wanted to make the team. Although, for the most part, I stayed within my comfort zone of sports that I'd tried before, I really wanted to make that team. I enjoyed the competition. I enjoyed pushing myself. And by the end of the week, I went beyond my comfort level and tried something I'd never done. I had a free two-hour block in my schedule, so I went over to the tennis courts to watch the team tryouts. I noticed all levels of players, and they drew me into the excitement of who won and which teams looked the best.

Over dinner that night, I told Amy how fun that looked, especially after having a chance earlier in the day to attend a demonstration for wheelchair racquetball. Once again, my long arms were an advantage, and I wouldn't go as far as saying I excelled, but the pro leading the demonstration said I had tons of potential. So, the next day, I went over to tennis practice after the team had been announced and offered myself as a doubles partner since one person had double scheduled and couldn't attend. I jumped in and participated in the hitting drills, practiced a few serves, and eventually played doubles in a few practice games. Now that was fun.

As I prepared to jump back on the bus and head to my next practice, the coach came over and asked, "Why didn't you try out for my team yesterday?" Not giving his question much thought, I simply told him that I had never played tennis before. He paused for a second and asked if I'd be willing to play on the team with one of the other players as his doubles partner. He finished up with "Never played tennis? Well, you do now. Welcome to the team!"

Weeks later, I received the good news that, indeed, they had officially selected and approved me as one of nearly fifty members of Team Navy. Unlike the Olympics, where athletes tend to specialize in one sport or another, they expected us to participate in multiple sports. I biked (handcycling for me since I simply didn't have the leg strength and stamina to peddle up hills) and did shot put, discus, rowing, and yes—tennis.

The selection honored me, but it excited me even more to get to spend more time with my new friends in the coming months. Navy adaptive sports created my first opportunity to spend time around other adaptive athletes, disabled service-members, and their spouses/caregivers. As a newbie in my wheelchair, I found it both inspirational and educational to talk with and ask questions of others in my same situation. We had no secrets or taboo questions in the group, and to say I learned a ton from my teammates is an understatement. Similarly, Amy learned a great deal from the other spouses in attendance about navigating the uncertain terrain of disability resources and emotional support. Just one year prior, before my accident, I would have never imagined developing such a close relationship with the people I met through adaptive sports. Despite our very different backgrounds, illnesses, injuries, and abilities, we had become family.

Each of the military services have their own adaptive sports program. However, somebody once shared their opinion with me that adaptive sports don't seem like a responsible use of resources. "It's just for fun, c'mon…" There is travel involved, facility scheduling, equipment, and the like. To the uninformed, that opinion may seem to make sense, but I can tell you as someone who truly benefited from them, formal adaptive sports programs are life changing. The people who participate in these programs have survived life-altering illnesses. They have recovered from injuries that have otherwise taken away their mobility as they once knew it. These people are survivors, and survivors react to those life-changing events in different ways.

Watching the other recovery patients when I was doing my initial physical and occupational therapy fascinated me. Just like in the hospital, there are some who come out in extremely dark places. They are emotionally broken and unable to bear the burden of what their new normal has put before them. The thought of living the rest of one's life in an altered state is, quite frankly, unendurable for some. So, what's the secret sauce that takes someone beyond all that? Purpose. A meaningful purpose and a network of friends, family, and coworkers who are associated with that purpose is an incredibly powerful incentive.

I know from some on that year's Team Navy that individuals in previous years had had an incredibly difficult time adjusting to their post-illness or post-accident new normal. Adaptive sports had provided a release or an outlet for those folks to refocus and had given them a new family with like-minded peers who knew their struggle. They truly had a similar story based on their "been there, done that" common experiences. Essentially, adaptive sports had given them something to wake up to every day and helped them set goals and restore a vision for the future. For some, adaptive sports were truly a lifesaver.

Although I never fell into a deep depression after my accident, adaptive sports did something similarly positive for me. It changed my frame of mind as I learned to do new things. It gave me challenges and helped me develop goals that would further my recovery and my independence. It pushed me to try things that I'd never tried before. In fact, I no longer considered myself to have a disability after my experience on Team Navy. Indeed, I knew nothing but ability. I'd discovered many new abilities.

It also gave me pause to reflect on that decision long ago at the Naval Academy when I'd allowed my academic advisor to tell me in convincing fashion that I couldn't play basketball and get the grades I needed. I regret that decision to this day. Instead, I look at life with a renewed optimism. My new motto has become: "Don't let anyone convince you that you can't do something. Show them what you can do." Life is all about ability.

With a new purpose and goals of competing in a meaningful way at the Warrior Games in Tampa, I found myself in a bit of a bind. I had nothing in Pensacola to fall back on in the way of practice. I didn't have access to a recumbent handcycle on which to train. I could use the rowing machines at our base gym, but I conceded to the mercy of Amy's schedule since she had to drive me there and help me strap myself in before I could row. I didn't have the special seated benches from which we threw the discus and shot put. But we did have a tennis court (and a sports wheelchair) across the street from our house. So,

I got creative and tried to do as much as I could without the luxury of all the right gear. Easy day.

Amy would go with me to hit tennis balls for hours. Although we were playing doubles format in the games, I worked on consistent serves and ball placement in addition to "chair handling" on the tennis court.

I also cobbled together a poor man's version of field practice equipment so I could throw shot put and discus in our backyard. Cobbled together is an understatement. As I look back, this is really a laughable memory. You see, the first time I practiced, Amy graciously volunteered to retrieve the shot puts and discuses after I threw them. I might add she did this in a typical west Florida summer, so she retrieved my implements in ninety plus degree weather, full of that ridiculous humidity common in Florida. She was a good trooper to help while I tried to throw from the confines of my wheelchair, but that only lasted one practice session.

"You're on your own after this" she told me.

No worries. Next time, I gathered all my gear and went out back with our two yellow Labrador retrievers. That was my first mistake. Since we had deep grass in the yard, I asked Amy to bring out my rolling walker. I could throw from the chair, get up and retrieve the implements using my walker, and do it all over again. I'd throw one shot put, and the dogs would chase after it (remember, they are retrievers). Since the shot put weighed eight pounds, they soon lost interest, but their instinct of chasing anything thrown by man kept them busy. It also slowed me down, waiting for them to find the eight-pound ball and remember that it wasn't worth their effort to try to get in their mouths.

So, I worked hard for about forty-five minutes and decided I'd step up my game and alternate throws between the discus and the shot put. Once I'd thrown all six of the implements, I'd use the walker to retrieve them. By this point, I had a good sweat going on and told myself that I'd get a few more throws in before calling it a day. I gathered one, two, then three of the discuses and realized that I really hadn't thought this through completely. I struggled to carry all three and got the bright idea that I'd put a discus in each of my athletic shorts' pockets. That way, I'd only have one to balance on the seat of my walker as I navigated the deep grass back to the driveway and my chair. About four steps into my walk, gravity took over, and those two discuses, along with my athletic shorts, laid on the ground around my ankles. Fortunately, I had on performance under-wear that went down to my mid-thighs.

As I stopped and regained my composure (and my shorts), I shook my head and laughed at the image some unsuspecting passerby might have had. "Hey, look at that guy. Isn't he the admiral? And aren't those his shorts down around his ankles?" Yes, with my new abilities, I couldn't forget that humility had to be a large part of my new normal. Fortunately, there were no passersby that day, and I swore my dogs and myself to secrecy that we'd carry to the grave.

Despite my feeble attempts to practice as best I could with what little I had, I couldn't wait to rejoin my teammates in Tampa. We arrived several days before the official opening cer-emonies to get acclimated to the south Florida weather (harder for some than for the folks who lived there) and to get used to the transportation coordination that took us to the various event venues located across the city. Television celebrity Jon

Stewart graciously served as emcee of the opening ceremonies and appeared at many venues around the city. I found it pretty inspiring to see how much time he spent talking to and listening to folks as well as cheering them on as they poured their heart and soul into the competition. I also found it quite incredible to see people from all services come together in competition, but the games didn't focus on winning medals—they focused on setting and exceeding personal goals.

I remember getting strapped into my rowing machine for my sprint competition and shooting to achieve a personal record. I'm sure many considered it quite the side show to see. Since I lack feeling in my legs and feet, I had athletic trainers first taped to my ankles (I tended to rub them raw and bloody if they weren't bandaged), and then I strapped my feet into the stirrups. All set, baby. Let's do this.

About that time, one giant of a man tapped me on the shoulder and told me, "Good luck, buddy." I gulped. We compete according to ability and medical classification—that way, nobody has an unfair advantage in competition. Well, this young man—easily half my age, twice my body weight in muscle, and I'll be damned, handsome to boot—sat in the rower next to me. An above the knee amputee, he strapped himself in, locked in his prosthetic, and prepared to go. Nope, that wasn't going to intimidate me. Legs as thick as oak trees? Who cares? Biceps bigger than both my legs put together? Doesn't make a difference.

Well, not so much. I've never been so wrong. During the race, in which he dominated, as I extended my legs on each stroke to create as much power and speed as possible, my knees kept locking up as I pulled with everything I had. Kind of tough to win a race against Hercules when I needed an athletic trainer to come help pop my locked knees so I could start rowing again. The rest is a foggy memory for me.

The entire two-weeks of competition were amazing, and to everyone's surprise, my doubles tennis partner and I made it to the semi-finals as unranked, unseeded nobodies. To our chagrin, the tournament organizer paired two Navy teams in the same semi-final bracket, and instead of both our teams fighting for the medal round, we knew that it was us or them. Only one Navy team would advance.

That other team was truly our "ringers"—prior team experience, lots of good tennis skills, and quite frankly, they'd crushed my partner and I every time we'd practiced. But competition breeds our highest level of performance. We fought a back-and-forth match, actually taking them into a sudden death tie break match point. We had the crowds going, and folks talked about this as the match of the century. (Perhaps that was only my wife on the phone with my kids, but still, a true nail-biter!) We ended up losing to an arguably better pair, but we'd given it all we had. I left the tennis court disappointed but fulfilled at the same time. After all, I did tell the coach, "I don't play tennis." I'm so glad he responded with, "You do now."

After a full morning of multiple tennis matches, I was immediately escorted to the track field. To my disappointment, I had to scratch from my shot put event since it conflicted with the tennis tournament, but I arrived in time to throw the discus. By early afternoon, I'd become a bit dehydrated from a full morning playing tennis in the sun, but I was still ready to switch gears and throw my best. The staff escorted my competitive group out to the throwing bench, and we waited. We waited. And we waited more in the blistering sun.

When my turn came to throw, I got strapped in and ready. The stadium seemed enormous, especially looking down range at a field that seemed to go on as far as the eye could see. *C'mon, mind your form,* I thought. *Visualize your best throw. Good hand placement, good rhythm, and let it fly!*

Each of my three competition throws went progressively further, and from my coach's reaction, I felt like I had done better than in any of the practices. The rules restricted the coaches to a distant viewing area, so they couldn't coach their athletes once they got on the throwing bench. It pleased me that I didn't have to retrieve my own discuses and risk losing my drawers in the middle of a crowded stadium. Life is good! I left the stadium ready for a gallon of Gatorade, a sixty-degree air-conditioned room, and few minutes of shuteye.

I got back to the hotel and wondered how my best throw would hold up with the competition. Now, I said that the Warrior Games are less about the medals and more about proving to oneself, one's team, and one's family new abilities. That's all fine, and it sounds good—that is, until you win a gold medal. I got that good (and surprising) news from our coaches at dinner and slept with a satisfaction I'd never felt before that night.

Two days after my medal ceremony, they asked me to do an interview for a local TV station. As that unicorn I described earlier, many folks wanted me to talk and do print, radio, and television interviews. I saw that as an opportunity and great platform for me to raise awareness, talk about the real value of events like the Department of Defense Warrior Games, and tell my personal story.

I launched into my message on the value of the games and how our participation wasn't necessarily about winning medals. The host of this specific morning show had heard that I'd received a gold medal in one of the field events and point-blank countered with, "So, that medal of yours isn't necessarily important?" I thought about that for a minute and reminded her that the sense of purpose, the competition, and the confidence in these events made for the real secret sauce behind the importance of the games. But, I said, "If you want to take my gold medal, you'll have to pry it out of my cold, lifeless hands!"

I went on to make what had become a very important point around my personal story. I expressed my gratitude that the Navy and our senior Navy leaders had allowed me to continue my service despite my life-altering injury. That decision wasn't informed by my mobility. They made that decision based on what I still had in my heart, what I still had in my mind, and the passion I still had for leading sailors and making a positive difference in their lives. I remained, firmly, in the proverbial fight.

CHAPTER 22

Full Circle—
The Next Chapter

What's done is done. What's gone is gone. One of life's lessons is always moving on. It's okay to look back to see how far you've come, but keep moving forward.

—Roy T. Bennett

I was never foolish enough to believe that I could wear a flight suit forever. With my retirement date set for July 9, 2020, I knew that this awesome career I had neared an inevitable end. As that date approached, I had no bitterness or regret and remained proud of what I, and "we," had accomplished in my thirty-five years of service. I purposefully choose "we" because I truly believe that, without the servicemen, servicewomen, civilians, and families who stood by my side and did the real work, "my" contributions were meaningless and insignificant.

I also realized that I wasn't ready to be done serving forever. Since my accident, I had really looked to make a positive difference for our Wounded Warriors. I worked closely with our regional office in Jacksonville, Florida, and made it clear to staff around the country that I had become ready, willing, and able to talk to seriously ill or injured servicemembers and their families. I wanted to help guide them through the difficult times similar to those I had experienced nearly three years prior. Regardless of rank or position, I just wanted to offer myself as a mentor and someone who understood what they were experiencing. I truly believe that God put me in my position for a reason, and just like I dedicated myself to making a positive difference in the lives of those who worked for me during my career, I wanted to open up and provide that same compassionate leadership to families finding themselves in different places in life.

As my retirement ceremony quickly approached, I received a message one day that I had been nominated and selected to receive the annual Department of Defense Disability Recognition Award. The award recognized the example of crucial leadership that I had contributed to our Navy, its sailors, and their families since my accident. I've never been one to hang my hat on awards or recognition, but as I thought about this one, I hoped that maybe, just maybe, I had made an impact on how the Navy thinks about disability as opposed to ability. In doing so, I just might have helped influence a different way of thinking about the true value we seek from our workforce.

I'd be lying if I said my final tour didn't take a personal toll on me. In retrospect, during my years of service, I'm not sure how many folks could say they dealt with as much adversity as I dealt with during our three years leading the Naval Education and Training Command. But then again, a wise man once said to never judge anything until you have walked a mile in another man's shoes.

I guess I just took each of the hardships I faced one at a time and never allowed the aggregate stress to get to me. I know for a fact that, looking back, I had an incredible team that helped me navigate through the quagmire of tragedy, uncertainty, and personal hardship. That team included my immediate personal staff (in Navy terms, my "front office"), other local military commanders, my family, and without a doubt, the local community. I won't mention anyone by name, but they all know who they are.

I will say that, in thirty-five years of service, I had assembled and built the most incredible team with whom I had ever served, and I relied on the professionalism, teamwork, and family-like camaraderie that we formed during our time together. I felt no need to assert rank or seniority into what the situation had called us all to do. That small family of incredibly strong officers and sailors resembled a Super Bowl team with everyone playing a different position and everyone performing a different role. When the whistle blew, we all shared a common goal, and nobody ever uttered a word when work took us late into the night. To this day, that brotherhood remains a family I will never forget.

By 2019, I really felt like I was back in the full swing of things. I had figured out how to balance work from the office, outpatient physical therapy three afternoons each week, and travel for ten days or so each month, visiting my various subordinate commands across the country. My injury wasn't anything that I ever expected to put behind me, but I had learned how to live and work within the bounds of my new normal. Relative independence, including a newly rediscovered freedom of driving with my new hand controls, absolutely invigorated me. Having to take my driver's test all over again like a sixteen-year-old did not.

However, that was nothing compared to what happened on December 6, 2019. It started out like most other days. I woke early to shower, shave, and get dressed so I could get into work and get ahead on the day's business with hopes of knocking off early so I could take Amy to "Flight Suit Friday" at the Mustin Beach Officers Club. There are many things in my career that I won't forget, and Flight Suit Friday sits at the top of that list.

Since every aspiring naval aviator begins their training in Pensacola, it's only natural to assume we'd have some sort of capstone event or celebration marking the completion of their initial academic training before joining their first training squadrons. In Pensacola, Flight Suit Friday is that event. Having successfully passed their final academic test (which is difficult for some), each young officer comes to the Officers Club on Friday afternoon with the other members of their class to celebrate. This is the first official time that each of the budding aviators gets to wear their flight suits in public. Each class has a unique patch that adorns their left shoulder, typically designed by the class as a one of a kind. Those patches are ceremoniously attached on an overhead beam in the club, joining the hundreds of patches that have been presented before them.

In addition to the prospective aviators, significant others and parents help fill the bar area to capacity. With people shoulder to shoulder, an uncommon energy permeates the club every Friday night. It's something that must be experienced to really understand the electricity. I always made it a point to work the crowd and not only meet the families who attended but also talk to each one of the young officers. "Where did you go to school, and what do you want to fly after you earn your wings?" always made for an easy icebreaker.

Every Friday, as we left the Mustin Club and headed home, we left with a consistent opinion: Our Navy and naval aviation is in good hands with impressive young men and women stepping up in service of their country. But before we left, there may have been a traditional drink—an Irish Car Bomb—that we used to toast good luck and success in the training that lies ahead at the end of the evening. Yes, we were in good hands.

Little did I realize that the events of December 6, 2019, would serve to cease that tradition of Flight Suit Fridays for months to come. As I laced up my flight boots before heading out to my truck, one of my staff members texted to the group that the back gate to Naval Air Station Pensacola had closed. In reality, it had locked down so no one could exit or access the base. At about that same time, the sound of sirens screamed in the distance. Not one, not two, but dozens. Something bad had happened, and from the sounds of the sirens, it happened on the base. News and information was hard to gather, but through a public messaging system to each of the employees who worked on base and the families who lived on base the direction came to "SHELTER IN PLACE." The words "THIS IS NOT A DRILL. ACTIVE SHOOTER. SHELTER IN PLACE," still cause my heart to skip a beat.

I called Amy who, at home in the main house and told her to get upstairs with our dogs and stay in place until I could figure out where things were happening. As much as I wanted to get into work, I didn't want to interfere with the police and security force response, In addition, since I had no idea where the threat was located, I didn't feel comfortable leaving Amy alone. In the coming hours, we learned that the shooter had entered the Naval Aviation Schools Command headquarters building, located a few short blocks from our quarters. That was ground zero for some unknown active shooter but other details slowly came in. Later that day, we learned that three young men had been murdered in one of my largest schoolhouses on the base—viciously assassinated by a ruthless killer whose motives remained unknown. Later that day, still forced to shelter in place, I received a call that provided information on the shooter. My imagination raced and my greatest fears began to churn. This could change NAS Pensacola forever.

We learned later that day that the shooter was one of our international students, training alongside his U.S. counterparts here in Pensacola and had come from Saudi Arabia. As you can imagine, this event impacted the lives of everyone on the base and in the community. A senseless tragedy of this magnitude triggers many emotions, and with the news that the shooter was a Saudi student, immediately questions came in regarding motive. My life, and the lives of many others became instantly consumed with a myriad of notifications, information gathering, and short-term decisions that we'd be forced to consider and make in the coming days. We had clear, yet complex priorities: make sure that the Navy notified the victim families and provided the best Casualty Affairs Assistance we could; provide grief support for the thousands of students locally who impacted with an unknown range of emotions; more fully understand the local threat and how that affected our ability to resume training when safe; and the consider the impact of this tragic event on future training, since we learned that the facility where the shooting had taken place had suffered significant damage.

We planned for local memorial services and funeral services to honor our fallen, and many questions still deserved answers.

In the coming months, I became consumed with daily briefings hosted by the Federal Bureau of Investigations. Having worked in the White House and seen firsthand the level of coordination between interagency partners, the invitation to include the Navy's base commander and me in their daily briefs made for a pleasant surprise. As their around-the-clock investigation progressed in the days and weeks following the shooting, they made us privy to law enforcement sensitive information critical to my decision-making processes as it pertained to safety, security, and the eventual restoration of training to each of the schools located on Naval Air Station Pensacola. When the FBI and the other agency investigators began to piece evidence together, it became clear that the Saudi shooter had been radicalized, and his heinous actions that day were likely terrorist related. It was exactly the worst-case scenario I'd dreaded from the moment I received that initial phone call.

The months following the shooting physically and emotionally exhausted me. We worked seven days a week, dividing our attention between family, sailor, and community support in addition to a flurry of policy-related questions from various staffs in Washington D.C. given the implication of the foreign student as the shooter. Investigators determined that the shooter had acted alone, which provided the only good news. The base commander and I had access to sensitive information on the ground, not necessarily widely available to policymakers in the Pentagon, complicating policy and Department of Defense decisions. Despite that information gap, we managed to navigate the sensitive branches and sequels that emerged from the shooting.

On January 13, 2020, Attorney General Barr publicly declared and classified the lone wolf shooting as an act of terrorism based on local evidence obtained by the tireless efforts of the interagency partners who had worked around the clock since arriving in Pensacola immediately after the shooting. The impact of that fateful day is still felt in Pensacola and around our Navy today. Nothing can replace a son or brother taken too soon by the random acts of a cowardly terrorist, but the mutual support that we witnessed locally in Pensacola (that resonated around the Navy and within the Department of Defense) allowed us to return to some sort of normalcy. Despite that, Naval Air Station Pensacola will forever be impacted by the events of December 6, 2019.

Healing and resilience come in many forms. Unlike the physical injury I continued to work my way through, the scars inflicted towards the families, coworkers, and community members associated with the terrorist shooting were much more emotional in nature. These were completely different circumstances, but there were a tremendous number of similarities in what I witnessed as our Navy training commands, the larger supporting Naval Air Station, and the community of Pensacola eventually moved beyond the impacts of the shooting.

I remain committed to my belief that the healing and resilience I've since seen firsthand resulted from the direct influence of a local culture fostered by the values bred into each and every future naval aviator, officer or enlisted. The toughness, togetherness, and sense of community—what I consider a hallmark within the Cradle of Naval Aviation and Pensacola—enabled each of us to grieve, pay tribute to our fallen shipmates, and eventually return to a critical mission.

In the coming months, COVID-19 would test our mettle further as the Navy, Naval Air Station Pensacola, and the Naval Education and Training Command dealt with the early stages of the pandemic. In early March of 2020, on a Sunday afternoon, I recall working through the day on a brief for our Chief of Naval Operations. We were tasked on short notice with providing an update on COVID's impact on our ability to ship new sailor recruits and conduct initial accession training at Naval Station Great Lakes, Illinois. Still uncertain of the long-term effects of this new health threat, I can remember thinking, "Won't it be great next month when this is all behind us?" Clearly my understanding—and that of most people—of the severity and long reach of the pandemic fell well short of what we learned in the coming years.

COVID provided another illustration of resilience, much different from the physical and emotional examples I've previously described. For perspective, the Navy's boot camp at Great Lakes serves as a critical cog in our Navy's manning supply chain. In a typical week, between 850 and 1,000 young men and women arrive at Chicago's O'Hare International Airport and are transported to begin their initial military training. That adds up to about 41,000 new sailors trained and graduated each year. Any significant interruptions to that flow of new personnel has a disastrous impact on manning operational ships, submarines, squadrons, and support elements around the Navy.

Despite my desire to flash forward a month and put COVID behind us, we quickly realized that the pandemic would not go away. So, given the mission critical nature of our new accession training in our single boot camp, the Navy asked us to do the impossible. How can you implement all the appropriate controls to minimize any exposures and outbreaks at the Navy's largest training command?

This became another great example of resilience that was architected in a matter of days. We would constantly monitor and adapt the plan and the protective measures implemented to ensure we protected the health of thousands of new sailors, instructors, and support staff. However, the fundamental bones of the program would rely on a two-week incubation period or restrictions of movement to ensure that we had no surprise cases of positive COVID infection that popped up during training.

My team in Great Lakes went to great lengths to address social distancing, physical fitness training protocols, face masks, and quite possibly hundreds of thousands of gallons of hand sanitizer. They also converted drill halls into isolation bays for anyone who ultimately contracted COVID. In addition, to prevent the unintended spread of infection from outside sources, the instructors willingly agreed to remain within the confines of the base for the entire eight-plus weeks of training until their class had graduated before returning home to spouses and children for a well-deserved break.

It truly inspired me to see the response, and the resilience, of a vital cog in our accession supply chain. No doubt the sailors and officers who made that happen remain heroes in my book. The biggest hero to me, a Navy SEAL, drove detailed planning and analysis to make this all happen. This is the same Navy SEAL who inspired me with the SEAL Ethos, something that, to this day, inspires me to keep going, keep improving, and continue to lead, regardless of my physical condition. No, I'm not a SEAL, and will never be a SEAL, but I am still in the fight!

As my retirement date approached, I had the good fortune

of receiving several considerations for what I might do after I hung up my flight suit. This presented new territory for me, and it seemed unnatural to think about the day I would actually face unemployment, so I probably had a false sense of urgency to land that next job. I interviewed for several positions in my final months (always mindful to do so on personal time as opposed to work time) and knew that, in my heart, I wanted to work for an organization that held meaning for me.

On one specific Zoom call, I told the prospective employer that I believe there's a difference between a job, which I defined as something more transactional in nature, and a passion. In my mind, I wanted to pursue a passion of mine so I could give back and contribute to something meaningful.

At this point, I went back and forth between two job opportunities, and as I described my job versus passion comparison, I realized the one thing I really wanted to do. After a few phone calls and emails, I convinced a particular chairman of the board I wanted a particular job. If he could get the needed votes of confidence and provide a formal offer letter that guaranteed I wouldn't be left hanging without an opportunity if it came down to declining the second option for which I'd been interviewing, then he had my commitment. I didn't question the salary or benefits. I knew the job, the organization, and the community and realized that this provided the passion I was seeking.

On July 9, 2020, I wore my flight suit for the final time. Due to COVID health restrictions, my ceremony was a weird hybrid. I was limited to having ten guests in the Blue Angel Atrium of the National Naval Aviation Museum in Pensacola. It was unfortunate that I could invite only ten in a glorious setting that can easily hold upwards of 5,000 guests, but that didn't diminish the significance of the day. I had my family in the audience. We also had two guest speakers, both current and former bosses, both instrumental in the decision that allowed my continued service following my injury in 2018. They shared their remarks over a Zoom call.

That day, I talked about a young, wide-eyed man who wanted nothing more than to serve as a Navy pilot. His journey started at Naval Air Station Pensacola in the place we affectionately call the Cradle of Naval Aviation. Ironically, for me, that journey had come full circle as I retired in the same place my naval aviation journey started in 1985. Even more ironic, I stood in my next "office" as I gave my remarks, having accepted a job offer to become the next President and Chief Executive Officer of the Naval Aviation Museum Foundation. I had found my passion, an opportunity to continue to stay involved in the legacy of Naval aviation.

As I'd learned in flight school and my early fleet flying tours, naval aviation breeds tough, resilient, and resourceful men and women who don't know the meaning of the word quit. I saw that same grit and determination in my son, who found out that same day that the Navy had selected him for instructor duty in Pensacola and that he would join us later that fall. That toughness, resilience, and refusal to ever quit was something I leaned on throughout my recovery.

Amazingly, I stood at the home of naval aviation—a home that had prepared me for the hardest few years of my life. The lessons I'd learned in flight school are the same lessons that our fathers and grandfathers who flew Navy decades ago learned. No flight goes according to plan. Always have a plan. Be ready to react. Take the circumstances you are given and never give up. Adapt, react with toughness and resilience, and stay in your personal fight.

Because of everything for which naval aviation stands, I'm a stronger, more independent husband, father, son, and leader than I've ever been. God puts us in situations that test our resolve but are never insurmountable. Trust in what got you to where you are today. I sure did. When I come to work every day in this amazing museum and get a daily glimpse into our rich history, I see stories of heroes and I hear the stories of folks who followed the same dream that I followed—to fly, to fight, to lead, and to win. Common people who willingly chose to do uncommon things. That's just who we are.

CHAPTER 23

Believe

Fans, for the past two weeks, you have been reading about the bad break I got. Yet today I consider myself the luckiest man on the face of this earth. I may have had a tough break, but I have an awful lot to live for.

—Lou Gehrig's farewell speech

Recently, I became one of millions of dedicated fans who watch a television show called *Ted Lasso*. The main character previously worked as a college football coach and accepts a job in England coaching the "other football" that we commonly call soccer on this side of the Atlantic Ocean. The current owner hires the coach because he knows nothing about soccer—all in a spiteful effort to make the team fail for a divorced wife who's left holding ownership of the club.

Ted Lasso seems to be a perfectly reasonable catalyst to make that failure a reality. However, Coach Lasso surprises everyone as a simple talking, storytelling, leadership genius. He's a master at building a team. He's an expert at cultivating and playing to individual strengths. He's creative at developing his players and instilling a sense of trust and confidence in each one, regardless of their individual talent or role on the team. And he's exceptional at using sports to teach life lessons to his team and in the owner's suite.

In one early episode, Ted hangs a simple yellow sign with a single word printed on it over his office. *Believe.* That sign reminds everyone in the locker room of the power of belief—belief in oneself, belief in the team, belief in ideals and goals. As a newly professed disciple of Ted Lasso and his school of leadership, I've discovered the word "believe" has incredible personal meaning on the journey I've taken over the past several years.

I've come a long way since that fateful day in 2018. I am by no means close to completing my recovery or declaring victory on my rehabilitation. My goal remains the same today as that first day in the hospital ICU. I am committed to walking again before this is all over.

I've had to relearn many things: how to get out of bed, how to walk with a walker, and how to drive with specially fitted hand controls (that one was a bit harder than the others since Amy proclaimed that, for my first six months driving, I was prohibited from having girls in the car with me or playing the radio loudly). My injury literally required me to teach myself or learn from others everything that most of us take for granted. But if you haven't figured it out yet, the word "quit" doesn't exist in my vocabulary. My mantra of #CozadStrong continues to drive everything I do. I don't profess to have any more strength than the next guy. I am committed. I am resilient. I am relentlessly positive. And I am thankful for my family, my friends, and my Navy for supporting me in those attributes.

Three months after my accident, I had the honor of talking

to retired Senator Bob Kerrey. During a work-related conversation, with the intention of centering on future training systems, our discussion wandered to my injury and how my recovery progressed.

Senator Kerrey served as a former Navy SEAL who was injured during the Vietnam War and was later medically discharged when doctors amputated his lower right leg as a result of wounds inflicted near Nha Trang Bay in the Republic of Vietnam. During our conversation, Senator Kerrey commented on how my positive attitude struck him, and he shared a philosophy that he first embraced after his injury. He said that, too often, people would comment, "In no time, you'll be doing everything you used to be able to do." However, the Senator looked at things differently. His amputation and, similarly, my injury really opened up a new perspective for folks like us. So, he said, "I am able to do things that I was never able to do."

That perspective offered an absolute gift and has remained in the forefront of my thoughts since our conversation. When I thought about that a bit more, I realized that, because of my injury, I'm doing things today that exceed anything I'd ever done before.

Since my accident, I've adopted five simple rules that reflect my ability to do things today that I never did before. These rules have helped guide my recovery and how I approach life going forward. Yes, I still think in terms of sports and competition because without competition, we'd all become stale and never progress to that magical next level. I never want to settle for good enough or become satisfied with where I find myself on any given day. In that sense, we all have the potential to live life as better people. We all have the potential to be better parents, spouses, and children. And in my case, I know that I have the potential to continue to get stronger along that path to my ultimate goal. With that in mind, here are my five simple rules:

One: Progress in life is measured in inches, not miles.

I still remember that first day with my occupational therapist when I checked into West Florida for my inpatient rehab. If he told me once, he must have told me a hundred times: "Forget what you used to be able to do and focus on what you could do that first day your comeback started."

I literally started over again from nothing, so the little victories—like lifting my feet off the ground four inches, putting my shoes on without assistance, or adding steps to my endurance each week—really added up. I take every seemingly small improvement as what it is—a victory and a step toward independence or normalcy. That next step provides what anyone with a significant injury on their own comeback strives to achieve. As Confucius once said, "It does not matter how slowly you go as long as you do not stop."

Two: Don't keep looking at the scoreboard; play the game for every minute and take enjoyment in everything you accomplish. The scoreboard takes care of itself at the end of the game.

As I've mentioned, I've always been a Type A personality, and before my accident, I didn't have the word patience in my vocabulary. I do now. I don't have a choice. My physical therapy team did a fantastic job helping me to identify and achieve short-term goals—things to work toward achieving in the next week or two. Goals like getting up those stairs into my house. Goals like becoming as independent as I've become in a few short years. Goals like getting out of the house for things such as working, socializing, and just plain living in our new normal.

Walking normally remains my overall goal, but I've realized that I'll face each one of those interim goals with the same energy that I give to ultimately walking.

When I played basketball, I never really focused on the scoreboard. I knew if we were ahead or behind but never worried about the point differential. Like most players, though, I could tell you exactly how many points I'd scored. I guess my approach today remains the same. I stay focused on scoring one point at a time. The good news is that I've been accused of being the guy who never met a shot he didn't take. With that attitude, eventually, we'll win the game.

Three: Nobody ever won a ball game from their hospital bed, so get back in the game and keep fighting.

We all have choices to make. Having had the opportunity to talk to many folks going through what I'm going through, I've discovered that not everyone commits themselves to recovery like I have. It's hard work, and frankly, it would be much easier to lay around and get used to living a very different life where you depend on others for everything you need. I won't let myself take that road.

Get out of the hospital. Become as independent as you can. Work to accomplish the seemingly simple things, such as putting on your own shoes and socks, getting dressed, and getting in and out of bed. Make the decision not to look back but to look forward to that new purpose you have and those new differences you can help make in the lives of others. Choose to keep living and to apply yourself to your purpose, regardless of where your recovery takes you and what that new purpose might be.

Four: Many games are won with a positive attitude and, conversely, lost without one.

I've never allowed myself to feel sorry about my accident or for what I can and can't do today. Yes, there are things I miss being able to do the same way I did prior to my injury, but I look to each and every day as an opportunity to improve. To take one more step than I took yesterday. To become stronger than last week. To appear more normal than folks thought possible last month. I continue to count the blessings along the way with a relentless positivity that there's still more I can and will accomplish.

I've come to realize that success in life, and recovery from an injury like mine, is realized by hard work and a positive attitude. But no matter how hard you work, if you don't believe in yourself and you don't let a positive attitude guide how you live your life, you're walking an uphill climb. Whether that climb takes you up Mount Everest or ten seemingly impossible steps into your house, you've got to believe in yourself and your ability to overcome whatever challenges lie before you.

Five: Everyone has a bad game or a bad day on the court. On those days, don't fear allowing your teammates to pick you up.

Even great ballplayers like Jerry West and Michael Jordan had bad games. Great athletes realize that basketball, just like life, is a team sport. The key to winning is knowing that it's okay to lean on others.

In my line of work, we learned independency early on in flight school. We prided ourselves on getting things done, and we're trained to do so from the very time we enter service. But I've learned that my new journey can't be accomplished without the love and support of my incredibly strong family. Or the healthcare professionals who continued to help me as much as my neurosurgeon following my six hours in surgery. Or a Navy that allowed me to balance my health and recovery with commanding a complex organization as a first priority. Knowing that I'm not on this journey by myself contributes to my relentless positivity. It's not only okay to lean on other people when life gets hard—it's often essential.

I'm familiar with a term commonly used to describe an individual's ability to recover—resilience. By definition, resilience is "the capacity to recover quickly from difficulties." I hear that word often in describing how our wounded warriors can and do fight back. But I also like to describe that ability to heal and make a comeback with another term—one that our Navy uses to describe four key core attributes that serve as guiding criteria for decisions and actions by naval leaders. That word is toughness. Because without that tough spirit, one will never become resilient. Without toughness, one will never find the inner strength to face each day with an understanding that it won't be easy, but the requirement for hard work that goes into each physical therapy appointment or just getting up and down the stairs is worth the effort.

Our former Chief of Naval Operations described toughness in the following terms: "Really, it's just our ability to take a hit, recover and keep going. To do this, we have to tap all our sources of strength. Whether that's the strength provided by rigorous training, the strength provided by encouragement from our shipmates and the fighting spirit of our people, the strength provided by our families reaching out to us—there are many, many sources of strength and inspiration. In the end, we don't give up the ship, and that's a measure of our toughness and resilience."

I have no doubt in my mind that I've benefited from a culture of toughness throughout my life and my career in the Navy.

My wife is tough. My family is tough. My Navy is tough. And without a doubt, naval aviation made me tough. Why would I let them down and be anything less than tough during this chapter of my life?

Before he departed on his very first deployment, my son spent a few days with me while I made the transition from the ICU to my inpatient rehabilitation hospital. He helped me get out of bed so I could go down to physical therapy. He witnessed my first attempt to stand up in that clunky machine. He watched me struggle to put one foot in front of the other and maintain any cadence that even closely resembled my first few steps. He then went home to join his squadron and head out for a seven-month cruise.

You've heard me mention how optimistic Amy remains in every sense of the word. Well, she told Dan, "Don't worry. When you get back, Dad will walk up and give you a hug when you walk off your helicopter."

I always cringed when she said that to anyone, let alone my son. In the back of my mind, I knew she only wanted to make him feel better about my condition as he left so he could concentrate on being the best pilot he could be. Worrying about Dad wasn't something that she wanted him dealing with. I knew that but kept thinking: Don't set up false expectations. Don't set anyone up for disappointment.

Well, after that deployment, he landed back at Naval Air Station Jacksonville on November 8, only seven months from my hospitalization. The distance I had to walk to greet him wasn't really that far—perhaps just over one hundred yards. A short walk for many other families waiting to hug their loved ones. You know what? Amy was right. Yes, I walked up on my walker and gave my son a hug right there on the flight line. Although it was just over the length of a football field, it was one of the longest walks of my life. She attributes that to the hard work and focus I invested since my accident. I certainly won't disagree, but I'll also suggest a magical healing power for an old aviator that came with just being on a flight line again. Regardless, that became another one of many awesome firsts that I continued to enjoy. When I tell that story, I come to the conclusion that Amy just might share my gift for having relentless positivity.

Another one of those crazy things that has been an amazing enabler during my recovery involved using the social media app FaceTime. Months after the injury, during a FaceTime call with my grandson Jaxon, Amy asked him if he wanted to see Poppa go up the steps. He instantly had an excited look on his face and fixated on the small screen with my image. As I stood up from my wheelchair, I could hear him in the background saying, "Whoa." As he watched me climb the first two steps, although I couldn't see the screen, I could hear him in the background. "I'm proud of you, Poppa."

How cool is that? He wasn't even four years old, but he understood how tough that was for me. "I'm proud of you, Poppa." Yes, the same kid who told Amy that "Poppa is slow-www," when I first tried to get around on my walker. But with inspiration like this, what else does a guy need to keep fighting the battle of his life? I'll share a secret with you. With support like I have, I think I'm in pretty good shape. Mount Everest, here I come!

AFTERWORD BY AMY COZAD

We are the sum of all people we have ever met;
you change the tribe, and the tribe changes you.
—Dirk Whittenborn

Inspiration comes in many forms. For some, it's something as simple as the sense of satisfaction for doing a good job. For others, it's a bit more complex; salary, job title, the importance of being a good parent, or perhaps an element of philanthropy factor into the many smaller elements that help motivate and inspire each of us in our lives. As I watched my husband progress through that excruciating recovery program, I witnessed his inspiration and motivation so desperately needed following that freak accident.

I had some apprehension when we hosted that large gathering of around 200 in our home so shortly after the accident. From the onset, I could sense Kyle's excitement. I remember him telling me, "I felt like a damn quarterback, putting on my pads and uniform, ready to get back in the game" as I helped roll him through the stadium tunnel (or the door of that temporary hospital room) and into the sea of flag officers and spouses.

I stayed close to his side that night, not sure how his stamina (or pain threshold) would hold up. It's hard to describe his feelings and the emotions of that evening, but despite being just six weeks out of major neurosurgery, he was among his tribe. Before we joined that virtual sea of visiting flag officers, dignitaries, and their spouses, I had urged Kyle to "top off" on his prescribed painkillers, anticipating that he'd regret the decision to spend even a few minutes with our visitors that night. But minutes turned into hours. Before we knew it, we had bid farewell to the last of the diehard partygoers nearly four and a half hours after I'd helped him come out to greet the group. Looking back, I realized that he wouldn't have traded a single minute that night.

At one point late in the evening, one of his staff came up to us and told us that the under secretary for the Navy wanted Kyle to come to the front of the house where he could pay his respects before he left. The narrow brick path and series of steps made that physically impossible for the wheelchair.

A bit tired and clearly feeling the searing pain caused by several hours of sitting upright for the first time in many months, Kyle quickly and politely said, "Tell the secretary that I can't come to the front. I'm in a frickin' wheelchair, so it would be great if he'd come back and bid his farewells where I could actually get around."

Standing nearby, I heard Kyle say that, briefly closed my eyes, and held my breath for a second. That's when the secretary came around the corner and politely said, "I had no idea." I can't remember who was more embarrassed, him or me. I do know it certainly wasn't my pilot!

I tell the story often that Kyle's tribe of aviation flag officers lit a visible fire in his soul that night. After going back into his room for the evening, I can assure you that, as I helped him back into his hospital bed, he told me that bed had never felt so good. I remember vividly how much his back hurt, so he popped another painkiller and watched TV for hours. The next morning, he told me that he hadn't been able to sleep because the event had so jazzed him and given him confidence that he could come back and serve with the support of that tribe. And you know what? That evening was the last time he took any painkillers for his back, against his surgeon's advice and estimated timeline. He was ready to move on!

A few short weeks after that huge party at Quarters A, after some difficult days at physical therapy and some other new hurdles Kyle faced, I could sense that his trademark positive attitude and happy-go-lucky way about life wasn't quite the same. He never came close to being clinically depressed, but he clearly wasn't himself. Fortunately, he married a gal who had come to know him inside and out. I knew when he was happy, and I could tell when he was out of sorts. Most importantly, I knew what made him tick.

That Friday, I'd had enough and had an idea that might snap him out of his funk. Kyle was lying in his bed doing some remote work on his iPad when I came in (he describes it as more accurately "kicking down the door"), both dogs in tow, with his flight suit, a clean T-shirt, and his brown flight boots. He was intrigued.

"Okay, mister. Put these on. We're going to the officers club this evening, and you're going to have fun!" As Kyle had learned throughout his Navy career, when anyone tells you to do something against your will and finishes with "and you're going to have fun," that's the farthest thing in the world from the truth.

But he was in no place to argue, so he quickly decided to give in and follow directions.

Now, for those not familiar with what pilots consider the most awesome uniform in the Navy seabag, I describe the flight suit as a fireproof Nomex "onesie" pajama for adults. Some would argue that not all pilots act like adults, but that's the gist. It's got a full-length zipper that makes it easy to throw on without most of the hassle associated with more formal Navy uniforms. Kyle says it's ridiculously comfortable, and the best part? He says it makes the wearer look "cool as hell."

Yes, easy to throw on in a matter of seconds—for an able-bodied person that is. I remember helping him that afternoon—much like dressing a baby on a bassinet. We must have wrestled around for thirty minutes trying to contort his legs into the right place while getting his feet stuck in a pocket every now and then. After a bit of a tussle, we pushed and pulled him to a point where we finally had it on. Okay, that wasn't so hard…until I realized that I'd forgotten to put on his protective shell. A few choice words later, I had repeated the process, and we prepared for the next challenge—flight boots.

I never thought much about the mechanics of putting on a pair of leather flight boots until I sat there staring at them, trying to figure out how to force Kyle's foot into a very prescriptive size twelve shape. He didn't even try to play the tough guy card and immediately told me, "You're gonna have to help me here, lady."

If it took me half an hour to put on his flight suit (both times), then it was easily double that effort to force his feet into those above-the-ankle leather boots. Every time we tried, his toes would curl up like a little baby's and we'd get stuck. I tried standing over him and pulling them up, standing behind him and asking him to push his feet into the boot, and even tried to pull them up myself.

I'd ask, "How does that feel?" And he'd always provide the same answer, "Technically, I can't feel anything, but I can tell you it looks weird." I didn't appreciate his frank honesty of "I can't feel anything," and the not-so-subtle sarcasm in his answer didn't help his cause. But finally, after taking a sharp pair of scissors and cutting a large slit in the side of the attached tongue of the boot, we were able to declare victory. That wasn't so hard, right?

By this time, I was out of breath and clearly perspiring (even though I'd convinced him early on in our marriage that "girls didn't sweat"). Whatever I was doing, I was gassed! So, more sarcasm from him, "Yeah, that wasn't so hard. Now, let's put on the other boot."

There are many times in our marriage when Kyle has told me that he really—and he means really—wanted to take back the words he'd said after seeing the look on my face, and this was definitely one of those time. He's quick to admit that, to my credit, I trooped ahead and finally got the second boot on. I remember how odd it seemed that we needed to rest for a few minutes after getting me dressed. He chuckled sarcastically at how he loved his new normal and declared victory by telling me, "That wasn't so bad. What do you say? Let's go to the club!"

As emotional and energizing as it had been during that big social event—that evening in a pair of surf shorts and a Hawaiian shirt—it had nothing on how he told me he felt putting that flight suit back on for the very first time. That flight suit represented an identity, and seeing him wearing it proudly, even if his toes were curled up awkwardly inside his leather flight boots, made me realize that he was back. I was looking at a changed man, ready to take on an unknown future. Rear Admiral Kyle Cozad was back!

It's crazy to think that something as trivial as a one-piece flight suit with a few Velcroed patches and rank sewn on could mean so much. But it did. I didn't give it much thought at the time, but looking back, that flight suit represented an identity and belonging for Kyle, much like it does for every other naval aviator who earns the right to wear one. The same identity and belonging that influenced his desire to continue to serve when he was a young lieutenant and we were considering a change in careers. The same identity and belonging that associated me with that elite tribe others call naval aviation.

Kyle and I have always had the "why" question in the back of our minds since the day of his accident and long-term prognosis in 2018. But we haven't let the why get in the way of moving forward, finding new purpose, and attempting to make a difference in everything we do.

My favorite story of how Kyle has made a difference relates to a young flight school student who recognized him as the "two-star admiral" as he rolled into the Mustin Beach Officers Club one Friday afternoon in the early summer. Kyle literally rolled in in his wheelchair that day for the first time following his injury. His flight suit covered that protective resin shell but made his shoulder insignia barely visible given the orientation and bulk of the shell. Regardless, everyone there knew exactly who he was.

At that time, so close to his injury and recent release from the hospital, Kyle remained somewhat uncomfortable spending time in public now that he used a wheelchair. But that Friday was different. The time had come for him to return to one of his favorite places—to see longtime friends and other new friends he'd not yet met. He relished being in his element, despite the fact that he couldn't yet drink a beer based on the pain medications he lived on.

The head bartender had cleared the floor in expectation of our arrival so Kyle could make his way in. As Kyle entered the main bar area, an old friend chanted, "It's the admiral. It's the admiral!" With that, old friends and new friends turned a welcoming round of applause into a rousing standing ovation. Emotion overcame both of us. I loved seeing him energized by spending time with friends, and as I watched him talk with people that day, I started to feel a returning sense of normalization in our lives that had been turned upside down.

As the afternoon crowd subsided, a young prospective flight school student came up to me, and while I'm not sure whether he knew me as "Mrs. Cozad," he asked me if Kyle was the admiral. "I've heard so much about him, and seeing him here in person is pretty amazing."

"That's him," I confirmed and mentioned in passing that Kyle was just happy to be able to fight his way back so he could continue to serve naval aviation and the Navy he loved.

In the coming weeks, I'd see the same young man not yet wearing a flight suit since he hadn't completed his classroom phase, and then again on his Flight Suit Friday, that rite of passage when each student has passed their academic portion of training, earning the right to move on to their initial training squadron and to wear their flight suit in public for the very first time. By then, that young student had become aware of who I was and always made it a point to ask, "How's the admiral doing?" Although I always offered to make a personal introduction, he remained reluctant and politely declined or made excuses that he had to leave.

Over a year later, after a long period of absence from the Mustin Club, I saw him again on a fall afternoon. This time, instead of wearing his flight suit, he wore his full dress white uniform. As the wife of a Navy pilot for over thirty years and the mother of a young naval aviator in his first fleet tour, I instantly noted the shiny gold object on his uniform—his wings of gold. I immediately congratulated him as he beamed from ear to ear. Then, he told me something in confidence that day that really put perspective on the "why" question we'd had since Kyle's accident.

He confided in me that flight school had been hard for him. Really hard. And on that first day that Kyle returned to a Flight Suit Friday, he had planned to terminate his training, contemplating a "Drop on Request," which would end his chances of ever flying Navy jets. He had convinced himself that it was just too difficult. But he admitted that, after seeing Kyle, his journey didn't seem as hard as he had once imagined. Watching Kyle that first day back in public and, in the coming months, seeing him progress as he became physically stronger served as his inspiration to continue in the program, working as hard as it took and doing whatever it took to become a naval aviator.

That Friday, he had reached the culmination of his training. He had achieved his goal and now joined the ranks of naval aviation with his coveted wings of gold. After telling that story, he hugged me and walked over to Kyle. He extended his hand and said "Sir, I'd like to introduce myself."

Looking back, that's the story that answers the question every time. Why? Why did this happen to Kyle? To live a life of purpose and make a difference inspiring others.

Kyle has adopted his own personal motto that he shares often with anyone who will listen. Don't let anyone convince you that you can't do something; instead, dedicate yourself to showing everyone what you can do.

I probably don't need to say this, but I will. I couldn't be prouder of my pilot!